22 years?
That's more than a life sentence!

18th February 1985 -15th March 2007

A TRUE STORY BY MICHAEL WOOD

Order this book online at www.trafford.com
or email orders@trafford.com

Most Trafford titles are also available at major online book retailers.

Note for Librarians: A cataloguing record for this book is available from Library
and Archives Canada at www.collectionscanada.ca/amicus/index-e.html

Printed in Victoria, BC, Canada.

ISBN: 978-1-4269-1226-9 (sc)

*Our mission is to efficiently provide the world's finest, most comprehensive book publishing
service, enabling every author to experience success. To find out how to publish your book, your
way, and have it available worldwide, visit us online at www.trafford.com*

Trafford rev. 8/15/2009

www.trafford.com

North America & international
toll-free: 1 888 232 4444 (USA & Canada)
phone: 250 383 6864 ♦ fax: 812 355 4082

Michael Wood

<u>The Author</u>

Michael Wood 53 years old and a retired Police Officer

All the names in this book have been changed. Not just the police officers but also the people that I dealt with. All the Incidents mentioned actually took place.

I would like to dedicate this book first of all to my wife Ruth. She has endured a lot over the past 11 years of being together and 5 years of marriage. I would also like to dedicate it to all of the police officers in the UK that have lost their lives whilst on duty and also to all the present serving officers. They have a hard job

I would like to also thank my two sons Anthony and Ryan who have loaned me the money to get this book published.

Michael Wood

The Beginning

They say that there is a time in your life that makes you change, the time in mine was 18th February 1985. That was the time I became the filth, a copper, the old bill call it what you like, it all means the same, a policeman.

I had served Ten years in the army from 1973 to 1983 and moved to Snettisham, Norfolk with my first wife and three children. I had done a resettlement course before leaving the army and decided to do the course for the police. This meant that I sat the exam for the police whilst in the army and once I got the pass mark I could then apply for any police force in the country depending on what mark I achieved.

Because I am not very well educated I got a mark of 125 out of 200. This meant that there was only a number of forces I could apply to, one was Norfolk hence the move there. So we got a mortgage and bought a house in Goose Green road, quite apt when you think I served in the army during the Falklands war. Although I didn't go as my regiment the 9th /12th Royal Lancers were in Germany at the time.

So mortgaged up to the hilt when the interest rates were 15% we moved and I applied to join the police. I was refused entry into Norfolk police as they had changed the entrance pass mark and I didn't have enough points. So I thought sod it I can just get a job and survive like everybody else does.

How wrong was I going to be? After numerous jobs, one working in a chicken factory, another as a kitchen and insurance salesman we lost the house so we had to move back to Northampton to live with my wife's dad. It was ok but after having your own home it was difficult living with an old man who was set in his ways. That's when I decided to apply for the Northamptonshire police, because I had already sat the police exam before leaving the army all I had to do was endure the two days of interviews.

Michael Wood

So there I was a 30yr old man with no actual qualifications apart from one, a good experience of life in the real world. Sat in Wootton Hall Northampton, the headquarters of the police, along with fifteen other candidates. Two days of hell that's how I would describe the interview process. There were fifteen of us both male and female, ranging from the age of eighteen to me. I was the oldest one of the bunch.

Every room we went into I noticed there were always fifteen real coppers sat around it. Each one of them was assigned to one of us. They weren't allowed to talk to us apart from tell us where to go for the next period of torture. What I did notice was, that when any of us spoke, someone would write on a clipboard. So I didn't stop speaking. I opened my mouth as often as I could.

There was a recruitment officer who was allowed to speak to us and he was very chatty, as I was the oldest and I suppose more mature than the rest he spoke to me a lot, asking me what I had done in life and why I wanted to join the police.

I of course didn't tell him the main reason was security for my family and the fat pension at the end, if I got to the end that is, and as I am writing this book you already know the answer to that question. So I gave him the bullshit that he wanted to hear, stuff like: serve the public catch criminals, make the world a safer place.

One reason I didn't give to him was the fact that I wanted to make my family proud of me. I wanted to wear a uniform again because wearing a uniform sets you apart from the rest and to some degree a uniform is like a force field around you, it does offer some protection and a lot of time respect. Even the real professional criminals give you some respect.

I remember two well-known brothers that used to live in Wellingborough. I was working nights and I had a Special Constable (hobby bobby as they were called, normal people that used to do a 9 to 5 job and then be a copper for the night, for no

2

Michael Wood

pay.) crewed up with me was a female called Haley. One evening we got a call about two men fighting.

But more about them later, back to the interviews. So there we were fifteen of them and fifteen of us, every time one of us spoke one of them made a note on the clipboards that they all had. Not knowing much about the system of interviews in those days, after all I was a thick squaddie. I guessed if I spoke as much as possible then it must help. But then again if I didn't know what I was talking about that would go against me. So I just made a point of talking to all the other candidates as much as possible, surely that would score me some points?

So after the two days we all sat in the corridor outside the Chief Constable's office and we were called in one at a time. I was the last one in the line, one by one they all went in and one by one they all came out. You could tell which of them had made it through by the look on their faces when they came out.

Out of the fourteen that went in before me only one came out with a smile on her face. That was Jan. She was about 25 years old, small and dumpy, but not fat. You could tell she worked out, as it was all muscle; she had a big arse that I always followed, (more of that later). My turn came to go in and as I got to the door the recruitment officer gave me a nod and wink, I didn't know if it meant I had made it or if it was just a sign to say nice knowing you. As I walked into the domain of the man who could change my life, I was shaking. My heart was pounding and I'm sure he would see it pounding through my suit jacket.

Michael Wood

The Chief Constable

The Chief was sat behind a huge desk made of solid wood. The carpet was heavy pile and felt expensive under my feet and right in the centre of the room was a lone chair. He asked me to sit down. I thought my knees would buckle underneath me before I got to the chair but I made it in time. He came straight to the point and said that he had read the reports about me and he liked what the recruitment team had said. He said a sentence that I will remember for the rest of my life.

" Mr Wood I would like to offer you the post of constable.
I am offering you a post for two reasons; one is your experience of life and the fact that you come from a bloody good regiment of the Army. You know as well as I that when you get to training school you will have to burn the candles at both ends to survive".
He wasn't wrong about that!

I walked out of the room and was met by John the recruitment officer who had given me the nod and wink. He shook my hand and said " One of the reasons the team had put you forward for the job was the fact that you spoke to all the other candidates, that was a good move, well done". We then went to the canteen to meet the other person who had got through, Jan. So out of the 15 only 2 of us got the offer of a job. Now the hard work really starts.

As I drove out of the headquarters complex I felt great and a bit nervous as to what would lay ahead.

Michael Wood

Training School Ryton-on-Dunsmore

Ok so I have jumped forward a bit, I didn't think you would want
to know all the boring stuff, collecting our uniforms and then
going to court and swearing allegiance to the queen etc, etc.

Ryton as it's called, no body uses the on Dunsmore bit, was like
an army camp on the edge of the town in Warwickshire. They say
that the first two years in the police are the most important. I
disagree. All the years in the police are important, it's just easier
for the top brass to get rid of you in the first two years, and so
the first two years is a massive test. I suppose the first test was
finding the training school and then reception. Because I had
served 10 years in the army I was used to a camp environment
and found reception straight away but there were males and
females walking around like lost sheep. Some were young and
some old like me, or older than the rest. Now I am old as I sit on
my balcony in Portugal over looking the beach writing this in the
sun.

Anyway I hear the distinctive sound of a pair of ammo boots,
(boots that drill instructors used to wear in the army) coming
round the corner. I looked toward the sound, waiting for the
person to appear wondering if the person would be the image
that I have in my brain of drill pigs. Tommy came round the
corner and the first thing I saw was the slashed peak of his cap.
(Slashing the peak is a process where the peak is cut at the
corners where it joins the cap. The peak is then turned down so it
no longer sticks straight out but actually nearly touches your
nose when the cap is worn.)

So there he was looking taller than he actually was, because with
a slashed peak you have to hold your head up so you can see
where you are going; his uniform pressed and his boots bulled,
I'll explain bulling of boots later. I looked at his boots and they
weren't too bad mine were better and safely packed in the boot of
my car and I would get them out later. Some more Sgts then
appeared they didn't make an entrance like Tommy just sort of
slouched round the corner.

Michael Wood

All of us new recruits stood around chatting introducing ourselves. I was looking at the females wondering which ones would be in the same group as me some were good looking with nice bodies. You know the type the ones that you could imagine being a stripper gram in a police uniform or a porn star. Two hundred, that's roughly how many of us were there. Our names were read out and we were asked to attach ourselves to a Sgt who held up his hand when our name was called.

There were 15 recruits from Northamptonshire police and when my name was called I noticed I was in the same group as Jan, remember her with the arse on my interview days. Our two Sgts who would teach us all about policing were totally different. One was from the West Mercia force, Griff and the other was from Norfolk, Rosie.

Altogether there were about 30 of us in my class; I say my class because I was chosen to be the officer that marched the class around from lesson to lesson. Each class had one and they were normally chosen as they had a military background. I used to be a drill instructor in the army and I was looking forward to teaching the class how to march. Griff said to me "Mr Wood can you get the class in some sort of order and follow me."

Well, have you ever tried to get 30 people of both sexes, of all different ages, (some who didn't know how to stand to attention let alone march) in to some sort of order? It was a nightmare but I managed to get them in a rough sort of squad, I would do a proper job later in the day. So we marched along behind the Sgt, I say marched it was more like a walk, as 75% of the class couldn't march. I knew then I had my work cut out getting them into some sort of order.

We arrived at a classroom and when we were all seated we had to stand up in turn at the front and give a brief description of our lives and what we had achieved. It turned out that I was the oldest, what a surprise after all I was 30. I started to give a brief outline of my life and what I had achieved and I must have been talking for about 15 minutes when Rosie stood up and said

6

Michael Wood

"Thank you Mr Wood. I am sure you could go on for hours but other people has to have a go".

Once we had all said our bit, some longer than others I was asked to choose a second in command to help with the control of the class. I looked at the class in front of me and saw that there were 7 women the rest were men. I chose a small slip of a thing. She was an Asian girl from the West Midlands force, great body, and one I admired every time we were in the swimming pool. I chose her, as I needed someone to get the rest of the females on my side when it came to drill. Griff gave me a strange look when I chose her but didn't ask for an explanation. Griff stood up and said that we should all fall in outside.

We all ambled outside and I got the class into some sort of order again. Rosie then said " Mr Wood I thought you were in the Army can you not do a better job than this?" Pointing to the class. I replied, " Yes I can Sgt but I need them all in uniform with their hats on to do a proper job." He seemed to accept my comment and said, " We shall see later then."

We were then showed the accommodation blocks, one for the male and one female and told if any of us were caught in the other sex's block we would be sent straight back to our own force and sacked. We were also told that during our ten weeks we would have a written exam on the Friday afternoons covering the aspect of law that we had learnt the previous week. If we failed the exam then we would take it again on the Monday morning before starting the next subject in law. If you failed three exams the centre would contact your force and ask the question, do you still want this officer as he or she has failed 3 exams?

It was then down to the officer's force to say yes or no. In my case I was lucky I failed 8 out of the 10 exams but always passed the re-sit on a Monday and always passed the practical exams so my force said yes.

The next day I got the class in uniform. It was kind of strange as we all had different coloured shirts on. My force wore blue shirts

Michael Wood

but a lot of the West Midlands forces wore white, the only people to wear white in Northants were inspectors and above.

Some of the women looked great in their white blouses and when I lined them up with the tallest person at one end and the shortest the other I couldn't help but look at the tits on some of them. Anyway I managed to get them in a correct squad for marching. I taught a bit but not a lot as Tommy the drill pig was meant to do the teaching in proper lessons.

I can remember the first day I marched the class onto the square for the first lesson with Tommy. He was there with his pace stick, (a pace stick is a stick that can be opened up to a given gap to get the distance of a pace correct during marching.) no good if you're a 5ft nothing female with a small pace or as in our classes case a 6ft 7in male with a pace of huge proportion.

I marched up to Tommy in good old military fashion with my own stick and ammo boots and presented the class. He looked at me, at my boots and stick and said very quietly in my ear so nobody could hear
" What's your claim to fame then?" I nearly said
"Just like you Sgt a drill instructor that likes shouting at people."

But I thought better of it and just said nothing. He replied
" I can see you have done drill before do you think you can win the drill competition at the end of the ten weeks?"

Apparently there is a competition between all the classes that have to do a series of drill movements devised by Tommy. I replied
" I have a good chance as anybody."

After a couple of weeks of drill the class were getting quite good but I wanted them better. Griff had told us that it was his last class at the training school and all the years he had been there his class had never won the competition.

Michael Wood

So one night after lessons I asked to meet all the class in the bar for a drink. They all had to attend as I was in charge of them and it wasn't completely social I needed to discuss the drill with them. We discussed the drill competition and as we had begun to gel as a team and getting to know each other better I put the idea to them that we do an extra thirty minutes drill before breakfast each morning and after class at night before dinner. They all agreed, some of them said they would do it if I helped them with the bulling of their boots.

I have mentioned bulled boots before. Basically what happens is you take a duster, wrap around one finger dip it polish and water and use small circular movements on the shoe or boot to build up a layer of polish, but of course as soon as you put the shoe or boot on and march the polish does flake off.

So I suggested that they all buy a second pair and keep bulling them for 15 minutes each night and they were only to be worn for the drill competition. Some of them complained that the footwear would hurt their feet, as they would be brand new. My answer to that was 15 minutes of pain never hurt anyone so it was agreed I helped with the bulling and we did the extra drill.

Life went on at the centre, we did our subjects each week, took the exam on a Friday I always failed it and took it again on the Monday. We did our practices about dealing with road accidents, death messages, and domestics, all manner of policing including attending court. We all went home at the weekends to see our families and of course we had fitness courses, this is where Jan's arse comes in remember Jan at the interview.

Well don't forget I was the oldest of the class, although I wasn't unfit the rest were fitter than me, so when we used to have the 3 mile runs Jan would say to me " Woody just follow my arse and I will get you round" slapping her arse as she said it. It worked I always got round the course because I was watching her arse the whole time and forgot any pain I had in my lungs or legs.

Michael Wood

Now swimming is another matter. I can swim like a stone straight to the bottom and you have to pass a swimming test, how did I pass, I didn't. I still got through, the reason I didn't take the test was luck. Two days prior to the swimming test we were playing inter class football and I broke my thumb. That meant I was in plaster for the test and couldn't enter the water so they passed me anyway.

There were three of us that couldn't swim in the class me and two females. One was a girl called Val, who was from my force and the other was my second in command the Asian chick with the great body. I used to look forward to the swimming lessons as we had to hold each other up in the water by our stomachs, and of course my hand used to slip some times as did theirs.

But of course as this was all going on, the day of the drill competition was looming. We had been given the format from Tommy and we practised every day after class. Every time we practised there were always mistakes, silly ones that would lose us the competition and I could see that another class was very good. I kept saying to my class " So are we, we can do this and get Griff the trophy" but mistakes were getting worse as the class were trying to concentrate too much. So I had a thought, two days before the competition I told them we would be doing no more drill.

Everybody thought I was mad including Griff who said "Woody I need to win this, it's the only thing I haven't won." "Don't worry Sarge," I said "you will win it that I promise." Although I was having doubts myself.

So it's the night before the big day. After the last lesson I asked the class to form up on the square for one last practice. They all started moaning saying we should have been practising for the past few days. I said "trust me I am a policeman" that well-known famous saying. They did trust me and we got onto the square and they all knew the moves and where they should go.

Michael Wood

I had borrowed a video camera from Griff and I filmed the whole event. I didn't tell the class why and afterwards I said that I needed to see the class in the classroom 30 minutes before the competition in the morning. Somebody asked about the film and I said all would be revealed in the morning. I watched the video that night in my room and noted down all the mistakes

The big day. I had asked the class to carry their best boots and shoes, as we would put them on at the last minute, as Tommy was going to inspect us. The whole class was sat in front of the TV and I played the video of the night before. I pointed out each individual mistake and said let's go. I was hoping that they would remember those mistakes and correct them and not have the time to introduce any more. It was a big gamble and I wouldn't know if it worked until the dining in night 3 days later.

So onto the square we marched. I presented the class to Tommy who was dolled up to the nines with his sash on and his gleaming boots. He inspected the class and commented on how well they were turned out and the standard of the footwear. That was a proud moment for me; I had turned a class of no-hopers into a disciplined group of officers on the square.

The competition went well and I didn't see any mistakes. When we came off the square the rest of them thanked me and said that it was a good idea about the video, they had enjoyed themselves. Griff was nearly in tears saying that was the best competition he had witnessed in all the years of being at the centre. I felt good.

Michael Wood

The dining in night

All of us were in our dinner suits and the girls in their evening dresses. We looked good and I still have the photograph of the class to this day. After dinner the camp commandant, (sounds like a concentration camp doesn't it?) stood up and started giving out the trophies for different things, best overall high marks for different subjects, trophies for the running, swimming, and sport competitions.

Our class hadn't won anything and Griff said to me
" All I want is the drill competition trophy."
Tommy then stood up and said that the standard of drill and turn out this year had been excellent and there was one clear winner with no mistakes at all in the drill competition, also the best turned out class. He then gave our class number I turned to Griff and said
" I told you I would do it for you" Griff was in tears and said
"Thanks Woody"
I then went up to collect the trophy from Tommy, as he gave me the trophy he whispered,
"PC Wood you are good, and a credit to your force" all I said in reply was
" I know".

As for the final exam, that covers all aspects of law we had learnt over the past ten weeks, and couldn't be re-sat due to there not being another Monday available, as the exam was on the last Friday morning before we left. We got the results in the afternoon. I passed first time with a pass mark of 95%. Not bad for a thick squaddie!

That Friday afternoon we all said our goodbyes and returned to the real world of policing, the streets, where the work really starts for the next two years before we are independent officers.

Michael Wood

3ʳᵈ June 1985

My big day. I left home and said good-bye to the wife and walked the short distance to the station in my uniform. I felt great and really proud to be wearing a police officer's uniform. I had achieved a lot in the past ten weeks at training school when, at times, I didn't think I was going to make it. But determination kicked in on many occasions as I always remembered what the chief had said at the interview, about it being hard for me. Well at least I proved to him that he had made the right decision.

So I walked to the station with a little bit of apprehension and fear not knowing what I would face in the future. When I got to the station a little Sgt called Colin met me. I couldn't believe he was a policeman he was only 5ft nothing. He stood there with a pipe stuck in his mouth puffing away. In those days we could smoke at work.

He said "PC Wood I presume", (I nearly said no Doctor Watson but thought I had better not push it on the first day.). He took me into the parade room to meet the rest of the shift and continued with the briefing, all about the crime the night before and who we had to look for.

The rest of the shift were experienced officers and voiced their opinions as to where you would find the suspects. Colin allocated the vehicles and tasks and I couldn't wait to get in a police car. But alas it wasn't to be. I had to stay in the station to collect my radio and be shown around so I knew where everything was. I was so bored following the dwarf Sgt around doing admin work, but I suppose it was a must before I was let loose on the streets.

For the first 10 weeks I was appointed a tutor Constable. The role of the tutor was to take me to as many as jobs as possible so I could deal with them all. (I became a tutor later on in service and it's a good job, no paperwork the probie (probationary officer) did it all.) So my tutor was Bob, so laid back I thought he would slide to the car and not walk. But he taught me a lot in those ten weeks.

13

Michael Wood

Ten weeks might not seem a lot to learn a job that some of them had been doing for twenty years, but in those ten weeks you also had to attend courses at headquarters for a week at a time, for in all, so the ten weeks became fifteen. I know the maths don't add up but you had weekends off after the week before returning to the station.

The weeks at HQ were called progress and monitoring, speaks for itself you were under the spot light again. Also there were more exams, on local procedure, as each force used to work differently. Now you know what I am like with exams, can't do them, but I can do the work.

Back at HQ I met the recruitment officer that I had met on the interview days, as he was in charge of the courses and set the exams. When he first saw me he said, "Welcome back. I understand you had a rough time with the exams at Ryton?"
I replied
" Yes I did but I always passed them on the second attempt"
"That's why we didn't ask for you to be recalled, as we were kept informed all the time on your progress. It was decided to let you continue as you were good at the practical stuff but not the written stuff."
That man helped over the next fifteen weeks and kept me in the job.

During the week at the course we had more input of law and had to sit an exam on the Friday morning. Those that failed had to re-sit on the afternoon when everyone else went home early. Guess who was there every Friday afternoon, YES ME I failed every single exam. The exams weren't difficult just a little ambiguous at times, as the law is. The tests were multiple choice and as I sat the exam again I used to sit there with my pen poised over the answer that I thought was correct, just before I applied pressure on the pen there would be a cough behind me, it was him the good Samaritan telling me it was the wrong answer.

If I didn't get a cough then I knew it was right. That's how I got through the weeks at Headquarters and I will always be grateful

14

to him. I saw him many times during my service and we always used to joke about the exams. He always said to me at those chance meetings,
" I did it because I could see a good officer in the making and I wasn't wrong."
 No he wasn't because I went onto be a well known respected officer that a lot of the younger officer used to ask questions of and I was renowned for my driving ability.

Michael Wood

4th June 1985

Back to the station, my second day. I promise I am not going to
write about every single day of my 22 years in the service. Just
most of them, the ones that are relevant, (good police jargon.)
including some that had a lasting effect on me mentally.

Finally I am out in the car with my tutor Bob. I have such a smile
on my face I am sure every person could see it from100 yards
away. I knew Bob could see it because he said, " well Woody, your
first time out I don't need to ask how you feel. I can see it, let's
go and catch some criminals." That was another turning point in
my life. I had changed from a man to a policeman, and it felt
great, a job I enjoyed until the last five years of my service, more
of the reasons why later.

They say that you always remember your first arrest and that is
true. My first arrest was a shoplifter. I can still remember the
actual name and the where and when it happened, obviously for
legal reasons I am not going to reveal all the details just the main
facts. Let's call the offender Gail; she had been to a well-known
supermarket in Weston Favell, Northampton.

She had loaded her trolley and walked out without paying. Now it
has always amazed me why people do the things they do. There
could be a number of reasons; they forgot, they were just
criminal, they had something else on their mind, or they just did
it for the buzz to see if they could get away with it.

On this occasion we don't know why Gail committed the offence
of theft. One thing I did learn from early on in my career, as a
police officer is that you can feel all the compassion and empathy,
but an offence is an offence. If you didn't do anything about it
you were in big trouble and eventually possibly out of a job, and
as I have said before I was in this job for the pension, which now
enables me to sit on my balcony in Portugal writing this book,
something I never thought I would or could do. I just woke up one
morning and said sod it I will give it a go, and if you're reading it
then I managed to get it published.

Back to Gail. Bob and I got to the shop and the security related to me what they had seen and I arrested her for theft, took her back to the station and booked her in. We couldn't bring all the shopping with us as evidence as there was £95.75 worth in the trolley. When we went through her property she had over £150 in her purse. She could have paid for the shopping, that's why I say it always amazes me why people do what they do. I won't tell you the outcome of the case or any others in this book, as I believe that would be illegal, and although I am retired I don't want to be on the wrong side of the law.

The rest of the day was taken up with paperwork. There was so much in the early years of my policing that it amazed me how we caught the criminals. We could be doing the paperwork for one crime and another officer would ask for assistance or we would be sent to another job, which involved more paperwork. So by the time you got to the end of your eight-hour shift you still had an hour of paperwork to do. That of course didn't help if you were back on duty in eight hours.

Some of the shifts in the early years were not good at all. We would start on a Wednesday after two days off, the tour would start at 1400hrs until 2200hrs, Thursday would be the same and then on the Friday we would have to start at 0600hrs, what was known as a quick change over. Some officers would sleep in a cell so they wouldn't be late for work the next day. The next three days were the same start at 0600hrs. On the Monday the start time would be 1400hrs again for an eight-hour shift, which would take you through to another quick change over on the Thursday. Basically it worked out that you did a week of early, followed by two days off, a week of lates then two days off and then a week of nights, then three days off. During that three-week period you would have two quick-change overs. (Confused yes, I was at the time).

So you can imagine what your body clock was telling you all the time, after a busy late shift, going home knowing you were on in 8hrs. You couldn't go home straight to bed, as you needed to unwind, tell your wives about your day, have a drink and then get into bed about midnight. You could never sleep knowing you had to be up in 5hrs. That's why the shift pattern was looked at in later years and they still haven't got it right 22 years later.

My first blue light run, what a buzz that was! In the early years we used the Ford Cortina or Austin Montego and they were known as an IRV -. Immediate Response Vehicle. After the first run I decided that it was the job for me. We were going to the report of an accident, not serious but the road was blocked. Bob put his foot down and then said to me
" What ever you do don't touch any of the controls, even if you think we are going to crash, don't touch the wheel, the handbrake, nothing, ok?"
"Ok I said."

I knew about the hazards of people grabbing the brake as somebody is driving. It's very stupid and dangerous. So there we were during a busy rush hour weaving our way through traffic. I was sweating but when I looked across at Bob it looked like he didn't have a care in the world. His eyes were everywhere, he was changing gear so smoothly, and unless you were watching him you wouldn't know that he had done it. Every now and then he would shout at a motorist as he was trying to get through the traffic. " You stupid twat or bastard" because the driver of the car had panicked and stopped dead in the middle of the road and frozen when they heard the sound of the siren.

If drivers actually read the Highway Code it tells them what to do if they see an emergency vehicle behind them or coming towards them. It certainly doesn't say stop dead all of a sudden from 30mph to zero mph nearly causing an accident them selves. I can't remember it word for word but it says something like: indicate to the driver of the emergency vehicle that you have seen them and when it is safe to do so pull over and let it pass.

Michael Wood

My first road traffic accident

When we finally got to the accident and I got out my legs were a bit wobbly, not because I was scared, it was the adrenaline that had been coursing through my veins. Bob said, "Woody just follow me round and watch how I play this. There is a system of dealing with accidents depending on how serious it is, ok?" First thing he did was make sure there were no injuries. The very first thing you have to ask on arrival, just in case an ambulance is needed. I looked at the mess in the middle of the road and saw that two cars had struck head on at low speed. On looking at the damage it made me realise what a killing machine vehicles are.

I was back to Bob now. He was chalking the position on the road of the vehicle and wheels, both radiators on the cars had been smashed and the fronts pushed into the wheels. Bob got in the drivers seat of one of the cars and started the engine. The owner of the car shouted out " Hey, you can't move that the radiators gone and the wheels are catching." Bob answered back in his normal calm drawl
" Watch me."

With that he started to drive it to the side of the road, with a screech of tyres and metal scraping on the tarmac. I had stopped the rest of the traffic beforehand; he then did the same with the other car. We both got the shovel and brush from the boot of the IRV and cleaned up all the debris off the road. I looked at my watch and saw the whole process had taken about ten minutes, and then the traffic was flowing again. We then had to interview both drivers at the side of the road to find out what happened and who was to blame. In those days we had to report someone for a traffic offence, even if it went nowhere when the papers got to the prosecution department. Now a day, if it's just a simple damage only, as long as both drivers have exchanged details and we have confirmed the details are correct it's left for the insurance companies to deal with. Obviously if its more complicated and there are serious traffic offences someone would be prosecuted.

Michael Wood

Back to my story, I keep going off the beaten track as they say but sometimes I think it's needed. Bob had interviewed both drivers and he had reported one of the drivers for traffic offences. He said "that's us done for now Woody, lets wait for the recovery truck and do the paperwork later." Paperwork later, that dreaded saying. Whilst we waited for the recovery truck Bob explained to me the process of dealing with a simple damage only Road Traffic Accident (RTA) right from the point of arriving and leaving the scene. We would come back later and do the measurements of the road when the traffic was lighter. "Do you think you can manage that ok?" "Yes" I replied, "good, the next one is yours to deal with?"

The recovery arrived and the drivers of the trucks got out and spoke to Bob as if he was a life long friend, of course he could have been as you get to know all the recovery drivers on your area as they normally attend all accidents to clear the road for you.

During the next ten weeks Bob and I went to every job that was on my list of tasks to perform. That's the mark of a good tutor constable; get as many of the tasks ticked off as possible, even if they are not always dealt with by the probie. Some may be too serious and it needed the know how of an experienced officer to ensure the evidence was correct, but at least the probie can see at first hand how the job is done and learn from it.

That's one of the most important things I learnt during my career as a police officer, there is always something new to learn. The reason being is that the law changes so much, that procedures have to change to compensate for it. I went to everything you can think of within the role of a police officer and learnt many things.

One thing I did learn that is very important, there is a saying run to a fire walk to a fight, that's not to say you go to a report of a fight as slow as possible, you have to judge from the radio message what the problem is and will it get worse if the police don't get there quick enough.

Michael Wood

That all comes with experience and of course knowing the place or people you are going to. We got a call one day about a disturbance at an address and Bob said, that's only so and so they fight all the time. It's probably a dispute with the man next door, they are always at it and when the wife of one of them calls they always escalate what is really happening. But you have to be mindful that the caller could be telling the truth about the problem.

So you still have to get there with some urgency. We started making our way and then we got a call from the control room saying that they had received another call and the problem was getting worse and that they had received calls from the neighbours claiming two men were in the street armed with weapons. On went the blue lights and sirens and away we went.

Now the blue light and sirens can have two effects on a problem in the street. The people can hear that we are coming; they can do one of two things. They can stop arguing and calm down or they can get more aggressive knowing if the other person gets the upper hand then we would soon arrive to stop it and of course we could get into a fight as well.

That's one thing a police officer doesn't want to do, not because there is always the thought that you could get hurt, but it's the paperwork that would tie you down for the next three or four hours. Most of the time the two people that are fighting would turn against the police and make a story up between them.

That's when it becomes stressful. You get somewhere, stop what could have been a serious assault and then have to explain yourselves to an internal investigation as to why you punched someone. This is one thing that really affects you mentally. Some would say they don't care it's just another complaint, but during the time that it's being investigated you are meant to carry on with the job as normal, go to other fights and domestics. At the back of your mind is, what shall I do here, do I get stuck in if someone starts or run away and call for back up, knowing if I get stuck in I might get another complaint.

Michael Wood

Also if I do get stuck in and get a complaint of assault towards me, it could lead to suspension and a court hearing. If any court rules against me, then I am out of a job. There is always the prospect of doing nothing, or not enough and you get in trouble for neglect of duty, which could lead to a heavy fine under the discipline code or even being asked to resign if it is found that you commit the discipline offence of neglect of duty a few times.

But for the force to ask you to resign they would have to be serious circumstances of neglect of duty. But how do you define the events to be serious? I suppose one way to look at it is that every employer has to abide by the law in relation to employment law and if the boss wants you gone they will do it within the confines of the law and find any excuse. I am not saying that the police force look for any excuse to ask an officer to leave, they just build a case against the person concerned.

Michael Wood

10ᵗʰ August 1985- walking the beat

So there I was, my first shift of independent patrol. I hadn't slept the night before, as I was excited about the prospect of going it alone. Of course you are never alone someone else would always turn up at a job if asked to do so and they would help you out with something. I got to the station 15 minutes before the shift started to get my radio and folder sorted out. When you go out on patrol you have to carry as many of the common forms as possible in case you have to deal with that offence.

It was a Saturday morning and there were a couple of hobby Bobbies on duty. At the briefing Colin sat at the front sucking on his pipe and gave officers their tasks and vehicles for the day. He turned to me and said " Woody you need to get your tit hat from your locker, (a tit hat is the large helmet that is worn by the police and not the cap) special constable Jones will then drop you off on the eastern side of town, you are patrolling the area for the day."

Walking, I thought I didn't want to walk; I wanted to be in a car going to all the good jobs. I got into the car with the special and couldn't wait to get out. It turns out he was 18 years old and had only just passed his test and it showed. I was unable to drive a police car until I had completed a 2-week course with the police driving school although I could drive anything from a moped to a 52 tonne tank.

I actually walked the beat for about 18 months, apart from the odd day out in an IRV and of course I didn't walk on nights, as we were always double crewed as far as possible. My skipper then said to me one Friday, "Woody next week you are on a driving course report to the driving school at 9 on Monday and make sure you have your licence with you or you won't be able to do the course."

At last I thought. Police driving course. I did the driving course and I was let loose on my own for the first time. All the reports from my skipper were good and the Chief Constable confirmed my appointment. I had made it I was a fully-fledged policeman, until you see the Chief and he confirms your appointment they can ask you to leave at any time and the only reason they need to give is that you do not have what it takes to become a police officer.

Now the only way they could get rid of me was if I did something criminal or I severely broke the discipline code and I had no intention of doing that. Now that I was driving I saw an interesting advert on force orders. Force orders came out on a monthly basis and contained different posts that were available, any transfers that were taking place and any changes in the law. The post being advertised was a general duties officer on the rural section.

I liked the thought of working in the countryside. I could learn about different aspects of policing, how to deal with farmers, pig licences, gun licences. One of the tasks that had to be performed every six months was the checking of the early warning systems in the village police houses. If a house was occupied by a police officer then they completed the task.

However there was one police house on the area that was empty. I collected the keys from the property services department and carried out the checks. As I was there I looked around the property and thought this would be a nice place to live.

At that time I was living in another police house on an estate near to Headquarters. It was 95% police officers that lived there with their families. As you can imagine some of the officers had probably been there for 20yrs or more. That caused a problem with the older kids on the estate. Because we were new in the area and my kids took a lot of stick and bullying. So I applied to move into the house in a small village called Walgrave, I got no answer and every time I chased up my application I was met with silence. Then one weekend my two sons, who were only nine and six came into the house in a right state. Some army kids that lived nearby had beaten them up. That was the last straw.

Michael Wood

Authorised Firearms Officer

But before I continue on that story let me tell another. Once I had been confirmed as a police officer, I saw an advert on force orders for officers to become an AFO (authorised firearms officer). I thought yeah I could give that a go I was in the army and I was used to guns, so I applied. I was given a course and enjoyed it immensely. Basically it was a course about shooting guns and tactics.

The role of an AFO was to hold the fort at a firearms incident until the USG (Uniform Support Group) got there. So the AFO would have to take charge and set up a place where all the officers could meet and plan what to do next. He would also have to assess all the problems that may be there at the scene. One of the tasks of an AFO is assess the building if the problem is in a building. He has to look at all sides of the property and note where there are any windows or doors. This would need to be done without anybody seeing you. Once this is done he could advise the tactical officer and save a lot of time, the USG could then decide how to enter the building if the need arises.

Now you have all seen programmes about the SAS (Special Air Service) on the TV, the best soldiers in the British army. These were soldiers that I worked with whilst serving in Northern Ireland. I applied to join but was turned down. Now the USG would decide where to enter the building to disarm the offender. In the early years they were not very good, but at my time of retirement they were good, they had the gas masks the skills and the training but they would never be as good as the SAS, they are the best in the world.

So I did the course and came first in everything, the shooting, and the tactics the lot. I was an AFO now. In the early years every station had a gun safe and if an incident involving a firearm took place an AFO on duty would be called upon to attend and assess the situation. Before attending the officer would go to the station and sign out a revolver from the duty inspector and attend the scene to begin his tasks before the USG got there.

Michael Wood

One night I was on duty and just about to go home at 4 in the morning when I got a call to attend the station and see the duty inspector. On my arrival he said there was a man in a house in a small village armed with a shotgun saying he was going to kill himself and anybody that came to the door. The inspector wanted me to go to the house and speak to the man because I was an AFO; I said ok could I sign out a gun please? The reply was NO just go there and do your job.

Now I tried to argue the point saying if he had called on my help as an AFO then I needed a gun, he said NO go and assess the situation and if I needed a gun he would get one sent out to me. I thought what a wanker, and I thought that of the man throughout my service, and still do to this day. So there I was I had an address and a name. One of the tasks of a police officer is intelligence and information before you go anywhere.

So I did some digging and it turns out the man with the gun was a man I went to school with and grew up in the same village, I used to play with him and his brother all the time. It made the situation seem a little better but the fact was you had a man in a house with a gun, he was unstable and he could shoot himself and anybody that walked up to the door, and the wanker wouldn't give me a gun. Because I was young in service I didn't argue the point and attended.

When I got to the house it was situated in a cul-de-sac. There was only one streetlight, and that light was directly outside the house I was going to. Great I thought, there is no chance of sneaking up to the house and having a look through one of the windows to see if the man could be seen. I needed to know what sort of gun the man had. Was it a pump action shotgun, a side-by-side gun (a shotgun that has just 2 barrels) or a rifle? The only thing to do was walk to the front door and knock on it, so I did. As I knocked on the door I stood to one side in case the man fired through the door at me.

I called out his name "George it's Woody, we went to school together can we talk?" I got no response so I tried again and eventually George answered. When he spoke I recognised his voice and I knew that I was dealing with the boy I used to play with years ago. He said "what do you want and why are you here?" I decided not to lie to him and said " I am in the police now and I am here to help you. There is only me out here, I haven't got a gun and I want to talk." The remark was met with a wall of silence. I repeated myself and I got a response, "if you want to talk the door is open come in." I then broke all the rules in the book of being an AFO.

I went in through the door. Basically I was now a hostage if the situation turned nasty. What I should have done was wait for the USG to arrive and brief them on the situation and let them take over. My job would then be done and I could go home to my wife and kids. But here I was in the hallway of the house knowing through the next door was a man armed with a gun. My heart was pounding and I was crapping myself. As I walked I talked, I couldn't stop talking
"George it's me Woody I am in the hall and I am going to come through the door to you is that ok?"
"Yes" was the reply.
"You're not going to shoot me are you or do anything stupid?"
 George said, "no, you wanted to talk, so come in and lets talk."

I walked through the door and what I saw filled me with horror. George was sat on a chair with two guns, one in each hand. He had a shotgun pointing at me, another one pointing at him. I assessed the situation in a second. The gun pointing at me was a single barrel shotgun, so I knew if he fired and missed he wouldn't have time to reload. The gun he had pointing at himself was a side-by-side shotgun and his arm was fully extended to reach near to the trigger.

He was looking old and I could see that he was in an agitated state. I thought what have I done, I thought of my wife and kids, I thought of anything, I didn't want to think of the gun pointing at me. George motioned for me to sit in the chair across from him. As I sat I was wondering if the USG were on the way and what would happen when they got here. George and I sat and talked; we talked about growing up together and life in general.

After about an hour George gave me the guns and we walked out of the house together, as I walked out I called out:
"This is PC Wood I am coming out with George and I have left the guns inside."

I didn't want the USG shooting me. When I got outside there were no USG just two beat officers and the Inspector, who had decided not to call for armed support. Now a days though the situation would be dealt with completely differently. I did the paperwork and went home. On the way home I had to stop the car I couldn't drive as I was shaking too much. All the thoughts then started going through my mind, what would have happened if he had shot me, shot himself, shot me then himself, who would have had the job of telling my wife?

I was then sick on the side of the road. I managed to get home without crashing the car and had a very large brandy. All the time the events of the night kept going through my mind, what would have happened if I had done this or done that. I was still shaking the next day when I went back to work, nobody mentioned the previous night and there was no talking about it, no debriefing. I just got on with my work and went to the next job.

But that was in the mid 80's. Now there would be debriefings, you would be asked if you wanted to talk to a shrink about what had happened and you would also be allowed a couple of days off. In fact if it happened now I wouldn't have entered the house!

Michael Wood

Back to Walgrave

Where was I, the kids had been beaten up. I still had the keys for the house after I had done the checks so I just decided to move in. I took four days leave, hired a van and completed the move. On the last day of my leave my old Sgt Colin turned up at the house, still with his pipe in his mouth. He said the Superintendent wanted to see me and I was to go straight to his office.

I thought, "Now I am in the shit". I got to the station and was shown into his office. We weren't alone; there was also an inspector with him. (If you ever went into an office and there were two ranking officers there you knew it was serious.) The super asked me sit down and said a simple sentence; " You have 24 hours to move out of the house back to the house you have been allocated." I don't know why I said what I said next.

"No I won't. I have been asking permission to move into the village house now for the past three months. My kids got beaten up three days ago and that was the last straw."

The Superintendent face went purple. I could see that he was mad.
"If you don't move I will move you" was his reply.
"Try it, as of this point I am now booking sick with stress."
I stood up and walked out.

I got back to the house and phoned the police doctor. I was so depressed the whole situation of the kids and the Superintendent put me over the edge. The police doctor came out and asked the normal questions and at the end prescribed me some anti-depressants. He told me not to move and that he would speak to the Superintendent about the situation. That was on the 4th August 1988. I didn't actually move out of the house until 17th October 2005. The doctor had signed me off for a month and then everybody got involved. Welfare phoned and came to see me.

Michael Wood

The Deputy Chief Constable turned up at the door and when that happened I thought that's it, I had come this far to be told I was sacked.

But that didn't happen. He was a nice man. He sat down with me asked what had taken place and why I had moved into the house without permission. I explained everything, about the kids, about my application, about the lack of response from the Superintendent and also the meeting I had with him.

What he said next was music to my ears.

"Michael, this an order from me. You are to stay in this house and when you are fit for work you can start at another station, ok."

I could not believe what he had just said.
"What about the Superintendent? "

His response was " Leave him to me, I shall be having words."
About a month later I started working at Wellingborough.

Michael Wood

September 1988 - Wellingborough

I will always remember my first day at Wellingborough. I was a bit apprehensive of working with a new set of officers, bearing in mind they would have seen my name on the transfer list on force orders, and telephoned their contacts in Northampton to find out why I had transferred. They would have been told the whole story.

After the first briefing my new Sgt, Joe (who I came to respect a lot as did he me) asked me to stay behind and close the door. I thought, here we go, here comes the pep talk about working there. What he said didn't surprise me. "PC Wood, I know why you came to transfer to the station and I will be keeping a close eye on you."

I started doing general duties in a patrol car and got to know the area, the officers I worked with and the local troublemakers.

It was Bonfire night1988. I had a female special constable crewed up with me and we got a call to say that two brothers were fighting on an estate in Wellingborough. (Remember the two brothers I mentioned earlier and the respect that some criminals give to the police.)

Well this was the time we got respect for each other.

I can remember walking through the estate and seeing two huge men standing toe to toe outside this house with a crowd of about ten watching. I walked up and said "Good evening." They both stopped fighting and the larger of the two turned round, looked at me and said:
"Copper you have two choices. Drive away in your police car or be driven away in an ambulance. This is a fight between two brothers on a family matter, none of us will make a complaint."

I looked at them and thought, no way am I being driven off in an ambulance. Besides, I have a young female special with me. I have got to consider her safety as well.

Michael Wood

So I walked away. I got the respect about seven years later when I had moved to another station. I had stopped at a chip shop one evening to get my supper. When I walked in, I saw this man in a wheelchair. I recognised him in an instant, he was one of the brothers that had been fighting.
I said "Hello."
He replied, "Do I know you? I have seen your face somewhere before."
I wasn't sure whether he would remember so I said
"I used to work in Wellingborough."
"I know you now, you came to the fight when I was fighting my brother."
"Correct," I said. "And you gave me the option of driving away in my police car or being driven away in an ambulance. I chose the first option."

"My brother and I have spoken about you over the years and you were the first copper to take our advice and let us get on with the problem between us. Because of that we respect you for it."
He then shook my hand.

I continued to see both brothers during my work and a couple of times they stepped in and said something to a group of drunks who were causing me trouble. One word from them and the trouble just walked away. I have to ask myself would they have stood up for me if I had tried to arrest them all those years ago, the answer I would certainly give is
"No."

Michael Wood

May 1989 – Immediate Response Vehicle Course

This was the month I decided to apply for an Immediate Response Vehicle (IRV) course. I was fed up with general duties work and wanted more excitement, more of a buzz. I always remembered the buzz of Bob driving me with his blue lights and sirens on. I was offered the course and started one Monday. The course was going to last five weeks and I have never worked so hard in my life. You might say that it was only driving, but it was driving with a difference.

First of all, you have to forget everything you know about driving. You were going to be taught from scratch by a qualified advance driver who had been teaching for years and must have had nerves of steel.

The first week was taken up with classroom work, being shown correct positions on the road for bends, roundabouts and other junctions. When to apply the brakes and when not to. Some of the rules were obvious when you looked at them. Only brake in a straight line. If you brake whilst going round a corner, you will never get round the corner. Another was always having two hands on the wheel when braking. That speaks for itself as you have more control of the car. That's why young joy riders crash going round corners. They don't have the control and are probably braking as well.

What about the highs of being a modern police officer, when I first joined you could have a laugh, there wasn't so much political correctness. When someone starts a new job, any job, there is normally some sort of wind up. The police in the 80's was no different to any other job. My wind up, I will never forget it I was sent to the centre of Northampton in the early hours of the morning, most wind-ups took place at night. There had been a report of a shop being broken into and the offender was still in the area, I had been given a description of what the man was wearing and told to go on foot and see if I could find him, well I did find him and I gave chase, I chased him all over the town, through alleyways, down all the streets.

Michael Wood

I must have been chasing him for about 20 minutes and I was getting tired I had told the control room every time I had turned a corner expecting another officer to catch him. I turned another corner to see the whole shift standing there laughing, one of them was wearing the jacket of the offender, it turned out as I had lost sight of the man, who was a policeman, he would then hide and give the coat to another member of the shift who would continue running me around the town.

16th July 2008 - Mum

I just want to sidetrack from the story of my twenty-two years a moment. Aren't mums wonderful! I am sitting on my balcony in Portugal typing away knowing I am running short of money. The job I was expecting to get is starting in the morning, a job I have been waiting three weeks for. It's only as a barman but it will help with the bills. So I phoned mum, asked her to call me back as I had no credit on my phone. I needed some money to see me through the next two weeks. She said she would put £50 in my bank. I said thank you and put the phone down, then burst into tears. I didn't want to ask mum, as she is a pensioner. The moral of this paragraph is never forgetting your parents. They will do anything for you to help.

Thanks Mum.

Michael Wood

May 1989 – back to the IRV course

Now I have calmed down a bit, back to the driving course. It was my wake up call to driving. I always saw myself as a good driver and the instructor said I was. I just needed to be made better. For the next four weeks three of us used to go out in the car with the instructor. We would take turns in driving. The drive took us all over the country and on some occasions the motorway. We would learn high-speed pursuit with a bandit car driven by another instructor, how to drive round bends at speed and also how to drive at a set speed on the motorways. We would almost never use the brake to slow down, just accelerator control.

The cars we used were unmarked but equipped with police radios in case of an emergency. On the rear bumper there was a small sign that said Police Driving School. I can remember one day I was driving along the M6 at about 100mph when my instructor said that there was a car coming up fast behind us. I slowed down to 70mph and took the centre lane.

This car pulled along beside us and I saw it was two uniformed officers in an unmarked car. They had obviously seen the plate on the back or checked the car registration via their radio. As I looked across, the officer in the passenger seat held up a clipboard with writing on.

It said, "Have a nice day and safe drive."
The car then pulled back. My instructor then said
"Lets go again woody"

So off we went at speed. Now, you may say, that it's wrong for us to drive at those speeds. But how can we catch the criminals that drive at that speed unless we practice? Not only do we train at those speeds but we also commentate. Next time you are in your car try commentating while driving. As you drive along, just say everything that your eyes look at. You will find that your speed will drop about 10mph as you are concentrating on the commentary, which is why the police train. I know sometimes it goes wrong and someone gets seriously injured or even killed, but then it's for the courts to decide who was at fault.

The day of my driving test. The instructors used to call it the final drive. They also used to call a hearse driving down the road the occupant's final drive. In a way it was. Every candidate starts with 100 points. As you drive, the chief instructor will not engage in any conversation apart from telling you where to turn next. Also as you drive along he will say the word 'commentate'. From that point you must begin commentating or you will lose points. You can be asked to commentate for 5,10 or 20 minutes. It depends on how good you are and how well you still drive.

From what I can remember, I think I commentated for about 10 minutes, although it seemed like a lifetime. At the end of the drive we stopped and he talked me through the drive itself. He gave me a mark of 98. He said " I never give any driver any higher than that." To me that meant that I had driven well and was one of the best. I got a grade 1 certificate.

On return to the station a few days later everybody wanted to be crewed up with me to see how I got the grade 1. They wanted to be in the car when we got called to an emergency and as I have said before, I was renowned for my driving. Even now, when I speak to my ex colleagues,
They still mention what new officers used to say about my driving.

I remember one particular night working the night shift. We had a call to a break in progress (burglary) and the Inspector was out with me.

The call was to premises in the middle of nowhere, so I drove how I had been taught. The inspector screamed the whole way, asking me to slow down. I ignored him of course, as I was in complete control of the vehicle. When we got there he said

"PC Wood, never drive like that ever again with me in the car."

Michael Wood

My reply was "That's fine sir, never get in the car with me again then."
He never did, but many people wanted to, so they could feel the buzz I felt in those first few weeks with Bob.

Now the buzz of driving fast through traffic with the blue lights on normally lasts about five or ten minutes depending on how far you go. I remember one night in March 1990 when the buzz lasted for forty-five minutes. I was on nights and another officer was crewed up with me. We heard over the radio that Bedfordshire police were chasing a stolen car and it was heading our way. I listened to the commentary over the radio and when the car was on the A45 dual carriageway heading towards us I started driving at about 30mph in the middle of the road. As I saw the blue lights behind me in the mirror I started to increase my speed.

I wanted to match the speed of the stolen car and slow it down gradually. These days you have to have special training and it's called TPAC (Tactical Pursuit and Containment) and of course the stinger wasn't invented. The stinger is a set of hollow spikes that you throw across the road to pierce the tyres of a car, allowing the tyres to deflate gradually. So I was up to 80mph and I could see the lights of the stolen car coming up fast behind me. Now there wasn't much room but the stolen car got on the nearside of me and rammed my police car out of the way. I managed to control the car and started to pursue the stolen vehicle.

As we were the lead police car, it was down to us to do the commentary. As I have said before, you say everything that you see and do. I gave the speed, the direction, how many people I could see in the vehicle and what they were doing.

Bearing in mind we were doing about 100mph along the road, I saw movement in the car. The sunroof was ripped off and thrown at us. I then saw a man stand up out of the sunroof and throw a small piece of scaffolding pole at us. The pole bounced off the front of my car and took out one of my blue lights. It could have come through the windscreen and taken us both out completely.

Michael Wood

The pursuit lasted 45 minutes and ended up back in the centre of Bedford.
The town of Bedford is in another police force area. As you go into another force area, you allow a local car to take up the position of lead car. That stands to reason, as they know the road and where they are going. Now throughout the whole chase the offenders threw everything out of the car that could be removed, the back seat, spare wheel from the boot, tools and toolbox, the lot.

We went through Bedford and the pursuit ended in a field. All three offenders were caught. Once again after it's all over you start to think. What would have happened if it had been different? The scaffold pole could have killed us both if it had come through the windscreen. At the time, there is so much adrenaline coursing through your veins you don't think of it, until after the event, and then you think WHY? Why did I do that, why didn't I do it another way? You realise that it is the buzz and the buzz is dangerous. As much as you try and forget the dangers, you can't. They build up inside of you until you crack and start hitting the bottle after work to try and forget.

Michael Wood

November 1989 leading to 1990 – first fatal

Now, I know I am jumping about a bit with the dates, but this was a bad time that has just come to my mind. I dealt with two separate fatal accidents and a suicide in a short space of time. A lot of people may have the conception that a fatal accident is the same as the other accidents, just more serious. Yes it is and it involves a lot more work. I am not going to tell you where the first fatal accident took place or the date, which would be unfair to the relatives.

It involved a van and a cyclist. Remember what I said about commentary during driving. The driver of the van would have seen the cyclist had he been commentating before he was blinded by the afternoon winter sun. I proved that in my report, which led to his conviction. Normally when you get called to a serious accident in a residential area, or a rural area for that matter, there is always somebody giving first aid. After all, someone must have made the 999 call. I got to the scene and a lady was giving first aid to the casualty.

I remembered what Bob always told me; "If there is someone giving first aid leave him or her to it, concentrate on what else needs to be done." This I did. I asked the person if they were ok to carry on and wait for the ambulance and they said yes. I then confirmed that an ambulance was   on the way and asked my control for assistance as I could see this was going to be a bad one.

The first thing at a serious accident is that you preserve any evidence. I closed the road completely. I was on my own, so I asked for the help of some onlookers. I got their names later and made sure they got a letter of thanks. Although the cyclist was there, there was no vehicle that had struck him. I asked some witnesses and they gave me the make and model of the van and said it had pulled into a drive further up the road. I couldn't leave the scene at that stage, as I had no help from other officers. The thing in the front of my mind was: drink driver and that I Needed to get to that house as soon as possible.

Michael Wood

The ambulance and help arrived. I explained to the other attending officers what I wanted doing and drove along the street until I found the make and model of the vehicle involved. I found a vehicle fitting the description parked on a driveway. Before I knocked on the door, I wanted to have a look at the vehicle to see if there was any evidence on it.

Sure enough, as I looked at the front there was a dent in the nearside wing and what looked like human hair on the bottom of the windscreen. I had a good idea that I had found the vehicle involved. I asked for recovery straight away, and asked that it should be a full lift. A 'full lift' is when the vehicle is lifted straight off the ground onto a truck without the wheels turning.

This would preserve any evidence if the driver tried to give brake failure as an excuse. I knocked on the door and the driver answered. He said that he had not seen the cyclist, panicked and driven home. My investigation took 2 months of taking statements, taking interviews and research. All the time I was being sent to other accidents and jobs. I eventually got the driver to court.

The other fatal I am not going to mention for a number of reasons. The main one is that I don't want to get into trouble, perhaps if I get this book published and seek legal advice I may be able to mention more in my second book.

The other event was a suicide on Christmas Day. All suicides and attempted suicides are tragic. I know this, as I have first hand knowledge of them, more later.

Now I could sit here and write about all the mundane stuff on policing and the incidents I attended, but the book is about me. The majority of incidents I write about are incidents that have affected me as a person and got me to where I am today. On a balcony in Portugal, sorry just had to get that in!

Michael Wood

Suicide

Suicide. Why do people do it, or even attempt to? I don't know, some people would say it's a cry for help or attention seeking. Nobody really knows. I certainly didn't when I woke up one morning to go to work and I turned to my wife and asked her if she wanted a coffee. There was no response.

I tried to wake her and couldn't. I checked her pulse and found that she was still alive, there was obviously something wrong and I called an ambulance. She was taken to hospital and spent a week in a coma. On the day she was taken in, I was beside myself. I didn't know what had happened and the doctors didn't know also.

It was only a couple of hours later when I had a shower and went to get a clean towel from the airing cupboard that I found the empty pill sleeves. I phoned the hospital straight away and they gave her the antidote. Why she did it nobody knows and I suppose nobody ever will. Perhaps it's an imbalance in the brain, I don't know why.

I contemplated it once.

We found ourselves, no that's wrong, I found ourselves in a lot of debt. I took out a loan to consolidate all the rest and found out that the interest was about 98%.

I could think of no way out and one day I transferred all the household cars into my wife's name and drove away. I drove to Norfolk where we used to live. I tried to find an isolated place to contemplate killing myself, at least my wife would have the insurance money to pay off the debts.

I couldn't find anywhere, as soon as I stopped the car someone would turn up.

So I booked into a hotel and sat there for two days with a bottle of pills and a bottle of whiskey. Obviously I didn't do

Michael Wood

it otherwise I wouldn't be writing this now. But even now I think what was I thinking, and the answer is, I don't know.

Michael Wood

16th May 1990 – boy racers

Of course, you don't need to contemplate suicide all the time, as the job can just as easily get you killed, as sometimes it does with tragic results. You read about it in the papers and it's always on national television if a police officer gets killed whilst on duty.

I was on duty carrying out a speed check in Wellingborough just down the road from a school. I had the radar gun trained on a vehicle that was coming down the road. Now I know what a lot of you are thinking, why am I persecuting the innocent motorist when I should be catching real criminals? Well, the answer to that is, the car was doing a speed of 79mph in a 30mph limit, near to a school. If your child got knocked down and killed by this lunatic driver, you all would say the opposite of the previous remark. You would say why wasn't someone doing a speed check in the area?

So, there I was, a car driving towards me at 79mph. I put my hand up to stop the car and when I saw it had started slowing down I stepped fully into the road. As the car got closer I recognised the driver as one of the local boy racers. All of a sudden the car accelerated and I had to jump out of the way to avoid being another statistic.

Now evidence is everything, so as soon as I picked myself up from the path I informed control via my radio of everything that had happened also naming the driver of the car. This radio call was recorded, as are all radio calls and the recording can be used as evidence.

I went straight round the house of the car driver, as I knew where he lived. I saw the vehicle on the drive, the bonnet was still warm and the tyres were even still hot. I spoke to the driver, who denied being out in the car. He said the car hadn't moved all day. I pointed out the car was still hot, he still denied it. I got another officer to visit the house and asked him to inspect the car and note down the facts down in his PNB (pocket note book). The case went to court and he was convicted and disqualified from driving, although that didn't stop him.

Michael Wood

Boy racers or Girl racers for that matter think they can drive, but they can't. A car is a lethal killing machine. I thought of saying years ago and I still say it now.

<u>"Accidents are caused by people not by cars"</u>

Now I am not going to explain my thoughts on the sentence. Think about it yourselves and I am sure you will come up with the same result as me.

A job came up in another part of the sub-division where I worked. It was seen as an exclusive job. There wasn't as much supervision from the bosses and the officers working the area created their own work and dealt with whatever came up. I applied, and because I was classed as an experienced officer with good skills and able to work without to much supervision, I was given the job, which was also an IRV driver.

Before I left Wellingborough, the shift organised a surprise party for me. Although I was still going to be on the same shift and see them from time to time, I was going to be at another station 6 miles away. Remember Joe the Sgt who said he would keep his eyes on me when I first got to Wellingborough? Well, he was the one who gave me the leaving present. He stood in the bar and said the following before presenting me with the gift.

" Woody, when you first came to this station you came under a cloud, and I said to you that I would be keeping my eye on you. Well I have and in the time I have seen you and worked with you, all I can say is that it was Northampton's loss and our gain when you came to Wellingborough. You have been an inspiration to all of the younger officers joining the shift and I am sure you will continue the work at your next station." He then gave me the gift and we both had a tear in the eye.

The reason I haven't given the new stations name is I am going touch on a subject that really affected me, professionally and personally. It was about 5 years later that my world fell apart and one person saved me. I will reveal all later.

Michael Wood

August 1990 – a new station

New station, new car, new area and new faces but still the same job. An IRV driver with a vast area to cover, most of the time on my own knowing if I asked for help on the radio it was a 10 minute high speed drive away. That's if they could drive as good as me.

New boy racers, every town has them, all of them driving around in their chipped killing machines. I remember one incident that I went to as if it was yesterday, an incident that will stay with me for the rest of my life, and an incident that still brings a tear to my eye as I contemplate writing about it. My Sgt was out with me in the car on this particular night and if he were to read this book now he would also remember every detail of the job.

It all started about 2230hrs. We received a call saying that there had been a serious accident in the town. On the a reported serious accident you have to think of what needs to be done as soon as you arrive, although things may change as soon as you get there. We were only five minutes away and as soon as we got there I said to my skipper Phil,
"I have a feeling this is going to be a bad one."

And it was. When we got there the road was clear. All the carnage was on the footpath. It's amazing how the mind works .I had to take in every detail in an instant and still think of what to do next, who to call for assistance, who to ask at the scene for help. When I say this I mean members of the public. The public are a great asset at the scene of an accident. There is always someone that wants to help, someone that wants to feel important, and most of all there is someone that you can rely on to do as they are asked. That allows you, the policeman, to get on with the work at hand.

There was a female on the pavement in a bad way. She was unconscious and bleeding heavily from a number of injuries. Rammed against a stone pillar, which was the entrance to a driveway, was a vehicle. The car had struck the pillar so hard that it was actually demolished. From what we could see and the road

45

markings and scuffmarks on the kerb, it was obvious that the vehicle had been coming along the road at speed, lost control and mounted the pavement hitting the female.

The driver was still at the scene in a bad state of shock. He would also have to go to the hospital and be interviewed at a later date. Before he was allowed to leave the scene I breathalysed him and it was negative. The ambulance arrived and the paramedics worked on the lady in the ambulance trying to stabilise her. The only other thing at the scene was a dog lead but no dog. I went into the ambulance and spoke to the paramedic who I had met loads of times at accidents that I had attended and asked him how the lady was. He said,
"Mick, she is in a bad way with multiple injuries I don't know if we can save her."
"Any ID? I asked.
"No, nothing".

Because there was no ID I had to start thinking. There was a dog lead at the scene, was she walking a dog? If so, was the dog lying in the hedgerow injured? Could the dog have a collar on giving a phone number or address? Also, was the lady carrying a handbag? Was that thrown into the hedgerow because of the impact? . We had to start making a search and I asked other officers to attend and help with this.

The paramedic stuck his head out from the ambulance and said that they had made progress with the lady and that they were making their way to the hospital. Away the ambulance went and we started the search of the area. One officer was in the hedgerow trying to find any evidence of ID when he screamed, " I have found something!"

That something was a little girl. She was dead and just about in pieces. So, the lady was out walking with a little girl and possibly a dog. I called for another ambulance and a doctor to declare the girl dead at the scene. We then got a call from control saying the woman had briefly come round in the ambulance and said a name. Wilson. She then went into a coma.

Michael Wood

After about 3 hours the scene was clear and we all went back to the station for a de-briefing and to put our heads together and try and come up with a plan of action. But the problem we had was that it was a Friday night and there was trouble in the town. Phil said to me that he would have to pull me off normal duties to concentrate on the accident. We had to find out that this woman and little girl were. Somebody, somewhere, was missing a daughter, a wife, and a mother, a sister basically a relation of some kind. Now the hard work really started.

Michael Wood

Investigating the accident

We had been given a name; it was actually an unusual name, not Wilson that's the name I have given them. The name could be of the dog, it could be a maiden name, it could be anything but we had to start somewhere and that somewhere was the phone book.

So Phil and I sat down and we trawled the phone book. We got at least 15 addresses of the name. We also asked control to do a voters check on the name and see how many more we could come up with. In total we had about 18 addresses. We plotted the addresses on the map and started with the ones nearest to the scene.

I think the hardest job of the police is trying to establish the identity of a deceased person. You have to knock on doors and ask the same questions. Who lives in the house? Who has gone out tonight and not come back? Do you own a dog? What were the people wearing that have gone out? All the time you are asking these questions the people are asking what is the matter, what are you not telling us? But you cannot tell them anything until you can establish you have the right address.

It becomes very stressful for them and you. As soon as you knock on the door of a house and the occupants see a police officer they fear the worst. The first question they ask is "what's happened?". Because of the circumstances we couldn't say. We could only say, "There is nothing to worry about. We are here on a routine enquiry."

We were there to try and find a family that had just lost a family member. So we had to start by saying there had been a serious accident and we were trying to establish if the person injured lived at the address, not even mentioning the dead girl. So we asked the same questions at 18 addresses and came up with nothing, apart from a few phone calls to the station from the households we had visited wanting to complain about us putting them through hell. Did they not think we were going through hell as well?

Michael Wood

We didn't clear the scene until about 0130hrs. We then had a meeting at the station and started knocking on more doors at about 0230hrs. Three hours later at 0530hrs and we had got nowhere. The woman at the hospital was still in a coma and not talking. What do we do now? The only thing we could think of was broaden the search of relatives to the next town. We may be able to find someone who has relatives in this town.

So, we started all over again with the phone book and the voters list By this time it was daylight and we had been at work nine hours. Nine hours of trauma and stress. You may think that knocking on doors is not stressful or traumatic but it is when the next door you knock on could be the one and then you have to deal with all the questions and screaming for answers, answers that you cannot give until the end of the investigation.

So Phil and I started again in a town three miles away from the scene. We had knocked on about seven doors and the time was close to 10.00 am. We had been at work 12 hours. We had one more door to knock and then we had nothing else we could do. We knocked on the door and this elderly lady answered. We told her we were investigating a serious accident and could we come in and ask her some questions. As soon as we said accident you could see the look on her face. We tried to reassure her that she may not be able to help us at all, but we had to ask the questions.

She showed us into the front room of the old house and I knew straight away that we had found a relative. Call it sixth sense or whatever you like, but I knew and by the look on Phil's face he knew as well.

But we had to go through all the same questions, but this time of course the questions were different, we weren't looking for someone from the house, we were looking for a relative who lived in another town.

We began by asking if she had any family in the area and she took a photograph of the side and said, "Yes this is my daughter and granddaughter." She gave me the photo and it was of a woman and a young girl. The thing that said we were in the right house was the dog sitting next to the girl in the photo. We asked a few more questions and came to the conclusion that we had actually found a relative of the dead girl and the woman that lay in a coma in hospital. What we couldn't understand was, why hadn't we found the home address of the woman. We then got the answer the name Wilson was the maiden name of the woman.

We asked the grandmother where her family lived and she couldn't tell us, but she could show us.

So we got into the police car and drove back towards the town. As we approached the area of the accident the old lady said, "that is the street." she pointed to a street that was 200 yards from the scene of the accident.

We had been going round in circles all night and the address we wanted was just down the road.

The next question was always going to be difficult. We asked who was going to be in the house. She said "probably the children." It turned out the injured woman lived alone with her 5 children.

I knocked on the door and a young girl of about 10, along with a dog, answered. She said hello and was very polite and then said

"I am sorry my mummy is not home at the moment. She went out last night to walk the dog and hasn't returned. I have got the children dressed ready for her. Am I in trouble?"

It turns out this little girl had got the children of the house up, she had fed them, bathed them and got them dressed. The youngest of them was only 18 months old.

I was so close to tears, as I am now writing about the incident.

The time now was 1130hrs the next day and I had been at work 23hrs.

Michael Wood

We got social services involved and handed it all over to the day shift. I went home and sat in the chair and cried for about an hour before falling asleep.

That was just one incident that got to me big style, and there are many more that had the same effect. They say police officers are tough. No we are not, we just have to give the impression that we are.

Mrs Wilson did make a full recovery, but she still had to bury her daughter. The person who was driving the car was a boy racer. He went to court and was convicted of death by reckless driving and sentenced to eight years in prison. Eight years is not enough for a life.

But, as I have said before, there were highs and lows. The majority of highs happened on the night shift, that's because you weren't attending domestic incidents or shoplifters. If you got a call about an alarm going off at a factory or shop, it could mean that there was a crime in progress. When we attended alarms at night we didn't use the sirens, just the blue lights and when we got close to the premises we would turn all lights off, including the vehicle's lights and coast the car in silently.

Sometimes I would actually stop about 50 yards away and walk in.

Crime in progress

A call came in. In the early hours of one morning, to say the alarm had activated at a local store. I knew the location, it was a row of shops on a housing estate. If I approached from one direction the road was very long and if there were a crime in progress, then a lookout would see me coming. So I had to work my way across to the other side of town and approach from the other direction, as it offered better protection from being seen until the last minute.

I was about 200 yards away and I killed all lights. I could still see to drive because of the street lighting.

Michael Wood

I then saw the lights of a vehicle coming towards me. I had to put my sidelights on, as I didn't want the car to run into me. If that happened then I would have some questions to answer. As the car passed I noticed there were three males in the vehicle.

I got to the shop and confirmed there had been a break in.

The shop owner appeared when he saw the police car. He lived above the shop and said that he didn't want to come down and try and stop the 3 men who had broken in, as he was on his own.

I thought, I wouldn't either. I would rather lose some stock than get a good kicking. I assumed it was the three in the car that had passed me. I viewed the security tapes and confirmed it was the same car. Although the crooks were wearing balaclavas, they hadn't covered up the registration of the car. A check was made and it was registered to well-known petty thief that lived just across the county border in Bedfordshire.
Now it's at times like this when you need an inspector with bottle, ours at the time did. Because of this he was well liked and officers would work for him. After a quick phone call to the station from the shop, (I didn't want to use the radio because scanners were big in the early years), the inspector said that we were going across into Bedfordshire's police area and that we wouldn't be waking up a magistrate up for a warrant as that would take at least 2 hours to get.

If we went straight to the house now then it would be classed as, in pursuit of offenders as the target house was only 15 minutes away.
In any case if there were a problem, then he would take the flak for it. Ten minutes later we were on our way, four police cars and about 12 officers, the whole shift nearly.

I asked the inspector, who was in the car with me,
"How are we going to get them to open the door boss?"
"Who said anything about asking? I am just going to put the door in."

Michael Wood

We got to the house and the inspector walked straight to the door and kicked it in. We all piled into the house to find three men counting the hundreds of packets of cigarettes they had just nicked from the store. Job done.

I settled into the new area very quickly and got to know the shift I was working with, one of them too close. I used to patrol on my own 75% of the time. The only time I usually had another officer with me was during the late turn: 1400-2200hrs. Because I was on my own a lot of the time, I was unable to complete the paperwork during my shift. I used to stay behind some days or nights. I would phone my wife and tell her I was going to be late. Eventually I saw this was getting to her. She wouldn't talk when I got home and stopped cooking me dinner, saying that she didn't know what time I was coming home so she hadn't bothered.

This obviously had an effect on my moods. That was when Rose began asking me how I was and started paying me more attention.

I was flattered. I was 38 and she was about 23 a slim blonde with a good body and great tits.

This is the one that I got too close to. We ended up having a fling for about 6 months and couldn't get enough of each other. Then it ended as suddenly as it had began, but we still worked together. This was in about 1994.

I am going to jump backwards to a couple of other incidents I attended on my own, incidents that put me in danger, incidents that could have had serious consequences towards my life and health.

Michael Wood

Domestics

Domestics – families fighting I used to hate going to domestics. I got a call one afternoon to attend an address were the son was causing problems with the mother and father. Although I had never been to the address, I knew of it from reading the intelligence reports. The only thing I knew about the son was that he was on drugs and liked fighting everybody that went to the house. This was one of those situations again. Do I wait for back up before going to the house and run the risk of serious injury to the parents or do I go in alone?

I decided to go in alone and hoped that help wasn't far away. When I got into the house the mother came rushing out saying her son was going mad and that he had a big knife, I thought "shit." But I couldn't stand there and wait for back up as the mother was going frantic. I informed control of the situation and asked for immediate assistance and went into the house.

At the time I wasn't a small man. I was nearly 6ft and well built. As I got into the house, I saw the father in the front room. He was hiding behind a chair. I asked where his son was and he said that he had gone upstairs to his room. I stood at the bottom of the stairs and called the son's name, he appeared at the top of the stairs with a Japanese sword and said
"Fuck off copper or you are going to get this!"

I was crapping myself. Here was a youth that was only about 5ft 2in but he was armed with a big sword. He started to walk down the stairs towards me and I backed into the front room. Just then back up arrived, a lone policeman. He came into the room as the sword-wielder came in the other door. I tried reason with him, calling him by his first name. He went mad, saying what right have I got to call him by his first name when I don't know him? All the time he was waving this sword around.

Now call me mad, but I decided that the only way to resolve this was to take him out. But how to, I didn't know.

Michael Wood

Then I got my chance. The other officer made a move towards him. He turned and started waving the sword around. I just jumped at him and wrapped my arms around the top half of his body, pinning his arms to his side. It worked. After a struggle he was taken away in handcuffs.
The thoughts then started hitting me. What if this had happened, what if that had happened? I knew then I was going to have restless sleep later.

But, amazingly, the one thing that came out of the situation was respect for me by the offender. He would cause problems over the next couple of years within the town. He wouldn't listen to reason from any other police officer. I would turn up and he would walk with me to the police car without any problem. One day another officer asked him, "Joe, why walk with PC Wood causing no problem when I couldn't get anywhere near you" The answer was "Respect."

"PC Wood was the only officer to take me down and if he says anything I will do it." Now that is weird, but you get respect from all sources, some of them bad, some good.

But of course sometimes you get no respect what so ever. I remember I was once again on my own patrolling the area and it was about two in the morning. I saw a transit van weaving all over the road. The driver had obviously had a few and I needed to stop him. As I followed I informed control as to where I was, as the van was heading towards the county boundary into another force area. I put the blue lights on and the van pulled over. Before I got out of the police car, the driver of the van was out and walking towards me. I got out and explained why I had stopped the man and as I could smell alcohol I would like him to give a sample of his breath, basically a breathalyser.

Well this man was about 6ft 4in and built like a brick wall. He looked at me, looked into the police car and said,
"You have no chance copper, there is just you and me and I am going to get back in my van and drive home."

Michael Wood

I thought, here we go, my back up is a good ten minutes away and I have got this man to contend with, how do I do it? The only way possible, grab hold and hang on. So I did, I jumped on his back, wrapped my arms and legs around him and screamed down the radio for help. It seemed like an hour before help arrived, but in actual fact it was only about 9 minutes. Someone drove very well that night to get to me. All the time I was waiting for help we were rolling around the street .I wouldn't let go and my arms and legs were hurting like hell.

As soon as help arrived the man stopped struggling and he was so compliant it was unreal. Once he was put in the police van that turned up I got back into my car. I couldn't stop shaking. Was it the fear or the adrenaline that was still coursing through my blood? I don't know. But it certainly opens your eyes as to what could have happened and you get to think why could it have happened. My only answer is lack of manpower, requiring me to patrol alone at night in potentially hostile situations. Not the forces fault, but the government's, for not providing enough money.

The next morning, when I got home, I couldn't stop shaking. My wife asked what was wrong, I said nothing. I didn't want to burden her with my problems. I didn't want her to see that the job was getting to me. I had a drink instead.

Back to 1994. Apart from getting close to the fit policewoman I also became close to a male colleague, not that way! We used to work together a lot and we knew each other's thoughts. I suppose that goes without saying when you work with someone for a long time. We used to start nights at 2200hrs and then at 0100hrs change into plain clothes. I used to dress up as a tramp, wearing a long wig, scruffy clothes, and carry a paper bag with drink in, but only coke or water. I had discussed this with my skippers and requested that no police patrols entered the town in question at all, for the whole night. I devised a simple code system to call patrols in if we needed them. This was my army training that had kicked in.

Michael Wood

The code system worked fantastic and I am sure it would work today even though they have digital radio systems. Someone, somewhere, will work out how to scan the modern police radio and you would need a simple system that would beat everything. So my best mate and I (let's call him Don) would go out on foot, not in pairs but a parallel route across the town. We had some good results.

I was sat in a doorway once and this car pulled up and a man asked me to be a lookout for the police. I just muttered something and the man got on the phone. A few minutes later another 2 cars turned up, five men got out with balaclavas on and they then started to ram raid a local shop. Unbeknown to them I was on the radio for back up. When back up arrived I didn't move and just left them to it. Six prisoners and three stolen cars. A good result, another high.

Drugs. I hate people who take drugs. They can cause a person to be either docile or violent but you have no way of telling which when you first get there. I was on my own one Sunday afternoon and I was sent to assist an ambulance crew who were trying to get a drug addict into the ambulance to take him to hospital. It wasn't in a house; it was in the middle of a street where the person had collapsed. I got to the scene and the man was on his feet staggering about in the road. Now, it was a sunny day and I had my shirtsleeves rolled up. I used to roll my sleeves up and made sure that I turned them up five times. They always had to be the same size and thickness on both arms, daft I know.

But I wanted to look smart at all times in uniform. I knew the man in question and called him by his first name. I managed to persuade him to go with the ambulance crew and was leading him to the back of the ambulance. All of a sudden his mood changed and he became very violent. He turned his head and sank his teeth into my arm. Luckily he bit into my shirt turn-ups, but I could still feel the pain of his teeth. He wouldn't let go and was biting down harder and harder. In the end I had to punch him in the side of the head to get him off. He was handcuffed and put in the back of the police car and not the ambulance. I asked for some assistance from another car to take him to the station whilst the ambulance crew attended to my arm.

Had I not had such thick turn-ups on my sleeves, I may not be here today. The man could have had HIV or any amount of diseases that druggies have. The turn-ups, had stopped the man breaking the skin, my arm was just bruised. Once again afterwards when its all over, you begin to think the what ifs again. I realised at that point that I didn't like confrontation and I would drive slowly to some jobs hoping another officer would get there first. I was becoming scared of the job.

Michael Wood

My first complaint from the public

Women. I used to hate going to jobs where females were involved. You had to be so careful in everything you said or did, or they could make things up and you could find yourself suspended for an alleged sexual offence. I remember one incident. Don and I were on patrol early one morning when we saw this car in front of us. It was about half past two. The driver obviously didn't know where he or she was going, so I put on the blue lights and stopped the car.

When we both got up to the drivers side of the car, we saw that it contained three females. I asked the driver all the normal questions. Was the car hers? Where was she going? Was she lost? She wasn't drunk but was being very evasive. We did a check on the computer and the car was registered to a different named person, not the driver. Because of this I gave her a ticket to produce her documents within 7 days, thinking of the offence of having no insurance.

She took the ticket and we allowed her to drive away. About 45 minutes later, we got a call from control asking us to attend the station and see the duty Sgt. As we drove to the station, we discussed what could be the problem. We even wondered if there was a special job coming up later that the Sgt wanted us to do. When we got to the station and walked into the office I saw the three females from the car that we had stopped earlier. They had driven straight to the station after we had stopped them and made a complaint of sexual harassment, saying we had made sexual advances towards them at the roadside.

I couldn't believe it. The sgt was saying that we had to apologise to them or they would take the matter further and we would both be suspended pending an investigation. I explained to the skipper why we had stopped the car and why I had given the driver a ticket to produce her documents. After about 30 minutes, we had to say sorry to the females or face an investigation. The driver then asked if she still had to produce her documents back in Cambridgeshire and before anybody could say anything I said

Michael Wood

"Yes you do, that is an official document that I have issued and if you don't produce them you commit an offence."

She wasn't happy and said that she may still consider making a formal complaint. At that point I had had enough. I stood up and said
"Do what you want, I don't care anymore, but you will produce your documents within 7 days."

I was livid. I felt like jacking the job in there and then, and then I remembered the reason I was there. The pension, I had to stay, so I did.

Two weeks later I got a fax from Cambridgeshire police saying the driver had no licence or insurance. Revenge was sweet, but there was still the stress of what could have been.

The stress was building and it was having an effect on my marriage and me. I was drinking too much after work and paying less attention to my wife and kids. I was getting home from work watching TV, drinking, going to bed and getting up for work again. A nasty vicious circle that was never ending.

But for all the stress there was the relief sometimes, when you could have a laugh, when you did a wind-up. I did one once on my own, even the rest of the shift didn't know about it.

Wind-up time

The police force has its fair share of jokers or wind-up merchants. New recruits usually suffer the most.

The Morgue Incident

Our force didn't do this joke. Another did it. As a result of it all wind-ups (jokes or fake incidents) were cancelled and any shift caught doing one got into trouble.

Michael Wood

Later on I shall still mention some wind-ups that were done by my shift, before this one was done.

Now this one was good. It took a lot of planning and involved a lot of people. Picture the scene. There was a new recruit who was being tutored. His tutor constable had spent days explaining about the wind up process and that an older officer from the shift was always doing them and that it was time one was done on him. So the plan was to organise identification at the morgue.

Yes, the morgue!

The new recruit was told that he would get on one of the trays. When the mortuary attendant pulled him out from the fridge and the sheet was pulled back, he would then sit up, scaring the older officer. So off to the mortuary they went. The new recruit got onto one of the sliding trays and was pushed back into the fridge. Now some of the fridges don't have dividing walls in them and the new recruit was actually lying next to what he thought were bodies. He was told that he would only be in the fridge for about 5 minutes as it was cold. So there he was, lying there waiting to be pulled out to scare the other officer .He started to shiver. All of a sudden the body next to him spoke and said
"Bloody hell its cold in here"

The new recruit screamed, sat bolt upright and injured his head on the floor of the tray above him. The older officer was in on the joke from the start!

Now I don't know if the story is a true one or not and I don't know which force did it or if it is true. But you have got to admit, if it is true, it was a bloody good one.

Back to the early years again. When we were on nights it was common practice for the whole shift to return to the station for a cup of tea at 4 in the morning. One morning everybody else was in the station. The controller asked, over the radio, where I was. I said I was en route to the station. I wasn't. I was standing in the back yard f the station. Now on nights we were allowed to park

61

our own cars in the back yard. I was standing in front of the controller's car.

All of a sudden I came across the radio, with some urgency in my voice, that I was behind a vehicle that was failing to stop. I started doing the commentary as if I were driving round the town. I could hear people running down the corridors of the station and then the rear door burst open. Out came the rest of the shift to back me up in the pursuit. When they saw me I motioned them to stay put and not say a word.

The controller kept asking for an update and asked if I could see the registration number of the car I was chasing.

I said that I couldn't and he proceeded to organise the shift sending them to different locations in the town. The rest of them responded in good form saying that they were all en route. After about five minutes, I said that I was now in a position to give out the number of the car. The controller asked for it so he could do a check.

I passed the controller his own registration number over the radio. It took about 30 seconds for him to scream down the radio that the car was his.

All of us were standing there, nearly wetting ourselves with laughter, especially when we heard the sound of running feet coming down the corridor towards the back door. The back door burst open and out he came. When he saw us all standing there he went mad and then went into a sulk for the rest of that night.

Michael Wood

Death

Death. I used to hate going to sudden deaths, but it was part of the job. I can remember the first time I saw death. I wasn't in the police. I was in the army; I was 17 years old and was at camp training to be a tank driver. Now, the Chieftain tank was 52 tonnes of iron. It was a Friday afternoon and my tank had broken down. The tracks been taken off and somehow it had to be pushed back into the hangar for the weekend.

Let me explain the gears on a tank before I continue. There are six forward and one reverse. To change gear you just flicked a little lever up or down with the toe of your boot, a bit like the gear levers on a motorbike. Also there is a separate lever that is moved by hand. This was contained in a closed gate and you had to lift the gate before you were able to push the lever forward or pull it back. These were the emergency gears and over-rode the normal ones. They were used if you wanted a constant amount of drive from the engine to negotiate steep inclines.

So there I was, sitting in the drivers seat of my broken down tank with the top half of my body sticking out the hatch. I had the handbrake on waiting for someone to tell me what was going to happen. Now what should have happened is that a rigid metal pole needed to be attached between my tank and another so I could be pushed back into the hangar. That didn't happen.

It was nearly 4.30 in the afternoon and people wanted to get away for the weekend. One of the instructors got into another tank and lined himself up in front of me/ Another instructor stood in between the two tanks and held a large railway sleeper in his arms. The tank that was going to push me back then drove slowly until the sleeper was in place and the instructor stepped out of the way. I was being pushed back no problem. The revs then dropped on the pushing tank and the sleeper fell to the floor. Now remember the emergency gears. They are used when constant amount of drive is needed. I heard the driver of the other tank say that he was going to put it in emergency forward.

63

Michael Wood

The instructor once again got in between the two tanks and held the sleeper. The tank was driven forward to take the strain so the man could get out of the way. All of a sudden the sleeper snapped and the two tanks actually touched nose to nose with the man trapped between 104 tonne of iron. As he got trapped, he was facing me and was about 3 feet in front of my face trapped by the waist. His face said it all. He was in severe pain. The tank pushing lurched forward again and again. I thought the trapped man's body was going to burst under the pressure. I let my seat down and dropped into the hatch out of sight. I then heard another soldier shout "Emergency gears"

Don't forget the tank pushing me was in emergency forward. When the driver selected reverse on the normal gears and put his foot down hard on the accelerator it didn't go backwards it went forwards. Because, I said earlier, the emergency gears over-ride the normal ones. When the tank was finally driven back I was frozen to my seat. I couldn't get out of the hatch for fear of seeing a man cut in half lying on the ground. So I pulled myself back into the turret of the tank and got out of the hatch on top and dropped off the back end of the tank. I walked away and didn't look back at all.

I can still see the man's face today. Perhaps that is when it all started, along with all the other deaths I saw in the army. Not just friends that got killed in Northern Ireland but the bombers that blew themselves up in Castlederg trying to plant a bomb to kill my patrol.

So I didn't like death. Now I can hear you saying, if I didn't like death why do the job, why not just leave? I couldn't leave. What else would I do? I have no qualifications to mention and then of course there is the reward at the end. I am now receiving the reward, but it has been at a cost. That cost is that I am sitting here alone and very lonely. I will tell you why later.

Michael Wood

Stress

I have already told you about some of the isolated incidents in my early years that caused a certain amount of short-lived stress. But, as my service went on, incidents became more frequent and more serious.

There were a number of incidents that started me down the long slippery slope to stress, depression and anxiety. It was the jobs I had to deal with and the danger I was in most of the time. I am going to touch on a few incidents now and as I have said before, the names have changed and I will not give the locations in order to protect the families.

I had dealt with many accidents during my career, but nothing prepared me for one I went to late one night. Once again I was alone. I received a report of a serious injury accident on a major road between two villages. Blue lights on and away I go. As I approached the area of the report I slowed down, because you never know what you're going into. Good job I did slow down, as I managed to avoid the first body in the road.

Now the scene of an accident is the whole scene. This one started at the first body. I had to park my car to block the road to protect the body and the rest of the scene. I asked control for assistance straight away and began to run up the road, where I could see some tail lights of a vehicle in the darkness about 100 yards away. I fell flat on my face over the second body. At this stage, I was starting to panic a little, not knowing what else I was going to find. Then I thought of the people at the car. They would want to see an officer that was going to provide help, not a blubbering mess.

So, I took a deep breath and continued. At the vehicles I saw a third body and the man who had been driving the car that struck them. Now he was a blubbering mess.

Despite this being a very serious incident, at that time I believe I dealt with the situation like any other previous fatal accident,

65

calmly and professionally. When I got home later that night I couldn't sleep. I was thinking about the accident and then I started thinking about other accidents I had been to. They all just kept going through my mind.

You know, it's amazing all the incidents I am going to mention and the majority of incidents were traffic accidents. It's that dreaded lethal killing machine again, the car.

I went to a simple accident. The report was that it involved two cars and there were no serious injuries. I arrived at the scene and saw that a car containing five young people had been hit in the side. I put my head in the car and asked if everybody was ok. I got the answer yes, but a couple of the girls in the back seat said they had pains in the neck. Now that is a warning signal to me of whiplash injury. I told them not to move and requested the fire brigade.

I needed the roof cutting off this car. I wasn't going to risk the life of someone by moving the girls from the back seat out of a car that was only a two door.

The fire brigade arrived and the top of the car was cut off. So there we were, three young girls in the back seat of a car, no roof on so we could monitor them and paramedics standing by with collars in case of spinal injuries.

I was holding the head of this young girl and talking to her. I explained that she needed to keep still and not move her head from side to side as she may have a spinal injury. She said she felt fine, but I insisted that she keep still until the paramedics can get a neck brace on her. I was talking to her about her school her family, anything to take her mind off the fact that she may be seriously injured.

I asked her another question and I got no response. I realised that she was dead. She had died in my arms so to speak, not a mark on her, not a sign of any blood, nothing. She was DEAD. How did I deal with that? I had about half a bottle of brandy when I got home, that's how I dealt with it and that's how I dealt with a lot of the incidents I went to that involved death.

But there's not just death as I have said before, there's the danger also. I can remember going to investigate a burglary alarm with another officer. We found a suspect on the premises. He was hiding behind a shutter door holding a hammer in one hand and a screwdriver in the other. I suppose because there were two of us it made him think a bit. He dropped both weapons and came without any fuss at all. Would it have been the same if there were just me? Nobody knows, but your mind does. You think about it all the time, the what's, ifs, and buts and I still think of those words today.

Lighter stories

Time for another wind up story I think, to lighten the mood a bit. Death, as I have said, some people don't like it at all. Paul didn't like it one bit. It got to the point where if he were asked to go to a sudden death he would actually come across the radio and ask if another officer could attend. He would even offer a month's wages for someone to do the job for him. So one day we set him up. We had the keys for a disused factory and got a dummy. We dressed the dummy and put an old man's mask on it. We strung it up in the factory, making it look like the man had hung himself. Cruel I know but you had to have some fun or you would go mad. In the end I did go mad to a degree. Back to the wind up.

So control asked Paul to attend the factory and the report of a man hanging. Now he came straight back across the radio asking if another officer could attend and even on went to offer a month's wages for someone to do the job. The answer was no he was the only person available and he would have to attend. Unbeknown to him everybody else was at the factory, hidden, waiting for him to get there. So he turned up, entered the building and started looking around.

He eventually saw what he thought was a man hanging and ran out into the street. One of us in hiding phoned the control room and told them what had happened. Control then come across the radio and asked Paul if he had got to the scene yet, as they needed an update for the doctor to attend.

Paul said no he hadn't got there yet, he was stuck in traffic and was there another officer closer? The response was no, he would have to go and assess the situation by himself. Well by this time we had removed the dummy and everybody was sitting in a group waiting for Paul to come back into the factory, and he did. When he got to the point where he thought the hanging man was, all he saw was a bunch of coppers laughing. He went mad and said he would get his own back in time. He never did.

Now you are probably asking yourself how can I remember all this stuff, all these incidents. A lot of the incidents I will never forget because I dream about them and sometimes wake up in a cold sweat. Some of the incidents need my memory jogging. To do that I have my pocket note books with me. The pocket notebooks are a written record of everything a policeman does during a day at work. It includes times dates and locations. Sometimes there may just be a few words to describe an incident; other times it may be five or six pages.

Now notebooks are kept for a certain period of time and after that time they are destroyed. Now I don't have the books for the first three years of my service, but I have the rest. I am reading them trying to find relevant points in my job as a police officer. Notice I don't say career, it wasn't a career it was a job. If it had been a career then I would probably have retired as a Sgt or Inspector. I just wanted to get to the end of my service and collect the pension and that is what I have done.

But it's amazing what a few lines in a book will bring back. I have just read one line in a pocket book and all it says is "1516hrs, 15-09-1992 A14 serious head on RTA (road traffic accident) hold the fort until traffic arrives."

That accident related to a driver who got to the junction of the A14 dual carriageway and instead of turning left he turned right.

Michael Wood

He thought it was a normal road and not a dual carriageway. He turned right as a lorry was coming towards him straight into the path of a car that was overtaking the lorry. A serious accident yes, did the driver die, yes, did it or does it effect me now, NO. Why I don't know.

Now I remember one particular incident that is not in my book, or I haven't found it yet. Remember that I said I used to dress up as a tramp and walk the streets. Well one night I was doing just that and a call came in from Bedfordshire police asking if we could attend a serious accident on their area. The town I worked in was on the border. One of the streets actually had a sign in it saying you were now in Bedfordshire but you wouldn't know unless you lived there.

So the call came in and I was the closest officer, in plain clothes, with a long wig on and in scruffs. I said I would attend. I had an unmarked car nearby with blue lights and sirens and set off. My partner, who was in the next street, said he would attend also, but he would go back to the station and change first and attend in a marked car.

I got to the scene and was dealing with the problem. It turned out not to be serious at all, but it was to the person who called it in. We had been there for about half an hour and it was about 1.30 in the morning when I saw this man walking up the road. Don't forget I was in scruffs with a long wig on. He was obviously on his way home from the pub as he had the usual small white carrier bag from a local Chinese take away.

So up he strolls on the side of the road where the accident is. Although I was in scruffs, I had my warrant card in full view on a cord around my neck, but he obviously didn't see it due to the amount of drink he had consumed. He tried to get past me and I asked him to stop and cross the road, he turned to me and said

"Who the fuck are you"?
I replied,

69

Michael Wood

"I am a copper and I am your worst fucking nightmare now get across the road."
He looked at me and looked at my mate who was in uniform, and my mate said to the man
"I suggest you do as he says or you will be eating that Chinese in a police cell."

Now I can have a snigger about that incident now, but what if he had called my bluff and started a fight. How would it have ended up? Would I be suspended for an assault because I wasn't actually in uniform and I didn't look like a copper? It's those three words again, if, what and but.

Back to the dangers of being a police officer. I have just read a note in my book that says 2220hrs; the day is the 21-01-1993 an officer has asked for assistance in Wellingborough town centre. Now the officer was well known to me and I worked with him a lot. He was and still is a good officer, very professional, very precise in what he did and always had a good attention to detail. That is everything a police officer needs for the courts. Now my notebook once again doesn't say a lot but I can remember that Bill was trying to restrain a drunken man for his own safety. He had done nothing wrong and wasn't under arrest.

But he decided to take out a knife and stab Bill in the upper arm. The upper arm contains a number of veins and arteries. The knife hit a major vein causing serious bleeding and Bill could have died within five minutes, if he hadn't received medical treatment. He did receive the treatment and he is still serving today. But that once again brings into play those same three words. What if and but.

Michael Wood

A dangerous one

My best mate Don and I were on patrol and we saw a well-known person who we thought was wanted, driving a car. We stopped the car and Don spoke to the driver. I confirmed that the driver was wanted and brought this to the attention of Don. Don said to the driver
" You're wanted mate."
"You're kidding." was the reply.
"No, failing to appear at court."

He was cautioned while still sitting in the car. Before anything else could be said or done he turned the key and drove off, with Don holding onto the door. Luckily the door was open and Don managed to crouch down on the sill of the car. The car door then slammed into the back of Don as it picked up speed. I jumped into the police car and gave chase.

I could still see Don hanging on to the arm of the driver. All the time the door swinging open and slamming again onto Don's back. The car went out of sight around a corner and when I got round, the offending car was stopped in the middle of the road. Somehow Don had managed to get into the car and into the back seat behind the driver. He was holding the driver round the neck. He wasn't going anywhere. We cuffed him and took him to the station. When we searched him we found a syringe with white powder in it.

Now I can hear you saying, "but that's part of the job, that's why you joined." To some degree yes, that is why I joined, for the buzz and the excitement. But eventually the buzz and the excitement turns to fear and you try and find any excuse to avoid a confrontation, or going to a possible confrontation. That's what was beginning to happen to me. I used to get home after every shift and go over the whole day's events. Then I would go over them again but with a different outcome.

Michael Wood

Sometimes the outcomes that I came up with were daft. Sometimes they had tragic results. It would still be going through my mind as I was trying to sleep. So I would have another drink.

Michael Wood

Getting injured and getting compensation

People talk about the knife culture now in 2009, but people have always carried knives. I have just read the details of three incidents in my notebooks where the offender we caught or stopped had a knife. Those incidents were over a period of four days. It's just that a person is more likely to use the knife today, that's why the police now have stab vests.

Of course if you are injured on duty, you can apply for compensation from the Criminal Injuries Compensation Board. You just filled a form in, attached all the statements of the incident and sent it away to London. After what seems a lifetime, and you have forgotten that you submitted the form in the first place, you get a letter back saying if your claim was successful or not. I put a claim in once.

I was sent to deal with a violent shoplifter who was causing problems at a local store. When I got there, he was still fighting with the staff. I got stuck in and as a result the offender broke my thumb. My skipper at the time told me to fill the forms in and send them away. I got a reply that said my claim had not been successful and if I wanted to appeal it had to be done in writing. The reason for the refusal of compensation was, they said, an offender had not caused my injuries during the commission of a crime and that I wasn't trying to arrest him. I was not happy, so I appealed. Eventually I was given a date to attend the hearing in London. My skipper had to come with me as he was the custody Sergeant on duty and he had made a note of my injuries.

The process of the appeal was like a court hearing. I had to sit in front of four people and justify why I was there. I was asked questions from a doctor about my injuries. All the statements of the incident were read out again and then I was asked to wait outside. After about 30 minutes I was called back into the room. The chairperson of the board stated that they had reluctantly found the appeal in my favour and awarded me £1500 compensation.

Michael Wood

What a farce that was, when you consider some of the awards that are made now a days. I am not saying I wanted more, I didn't, and it was the fact that I had to attend the appeal in the first place, that was the farce of it all. So far as I know this is still the system.

Michael Wood

Working alone

One of the main problems of working alone in a rural area is that you normally get to an incident at least ten minutes before anyone else. I can remember being sent to a report of a possible fatal accident on the A6 towards Bedford. It was a winter's night and the report was that a car had hit a pedestrian. I was given a rough location and from what they said on the radio I knew the section of road I was going to. It was a very fast section of road and it was unlit. If a car had hit a pedestrian, then the person would probably be a mess, and I wasn't looking forward to seeing the mess.

As I rounded a bend at speed with my blue lights on, I saw the location in the distance. It was where I thought it would be, there are some houses on one side of the road, but it was still a fast section. I could see at least four sets of hazard warning lights as I approached and I asked for some back up to make for the scene. The thoughts then started going through my mind. What am I going to find, will I be able to hold it all together and look professional, will I be able to take control of the scene straight away?

But usually when you get there, everything becomes automatic. However, on this occasion, it wasn't going to be like that. I was slowing down and the first thing I noticed was the amount of vehicles there. There must have been about fifty, parked on both sides of the road, another car was in the middle of the road with its hazard lights on. I assumed this was the car that may have struck the person. As soon as I got out of my car, I was mobbed by at least twenty people. They were shouting at me and pointing to the car in the road. I couldn't even get through them and update the control room as to what had actually happened.

The crowd then turned their attention to the car in the middle of the road. They all crowded round it and began rocking it. I called for immediate assistance and started pulling them away from the car. When I got to the driver's door, I saw a female in the drivers seat. She was in a deep state of shock. The doors of the car were locked, the windscreen of the car was smashed and you could see the tell tale signs that a person's head hat hit it.

But I still had no casualty. I stopped one man shouting at me and asked where the casualty was. He pointed to a house. Now I still didn't know if it was a fatal or just serious injury. One thing I did know is that I had to get the driver out of the car and into mine before the mob lynched her. I managed to get her out with some coaxing and walked her to the rear of my car, all the time being pushed by the mob. I was beginning to panic inside, but I couldn't show it. If I had, then all would be lost and I would lose control.

I got the female into the back of my car and as I closed the door I heard the welcome sound of the sirens, at last back up was here. Now I could start on the scene and try and find out what had happened and also why there were al least 50 people there, if you include the ones I later found in the house.

I managed to get into the house where the casualty was just as the ambulance turned up. Good, I thought, at least I don't have to deal with the mess. Although there wasn't a lot of mess, as the person's head had been wrapped up in towels. The amount of deep red blood that was seeping through the towels told me it would probably end up as a fatal accident. The person also had what looked like multiple fractures, but then who wouldn't if you were it by a car that could have been travelling at 60mph. I thought, great, this is another one for the memory bank, another one that I would think about when I got home, going over in my mind what could have happened. I wasn't looking forward to the thought of it all.

I did find out what had happened though. It turned out that there was an important religious man at the house and the people that were there to visit him have to join hands as they enter the house. The people that had parked their minibus on the opposite side of the road, joined hands and walked across the road first, straight into the path of the car. The person that had been struck had been at the end of the line. Thank God the car hadn't hit the middle of the line, then it would have been a lot different, one of my thoughts when I got home.

But you always think of the what, ifs and buts. I was working the early shift one day and was due to finish at 2pm. It had been a quiet morning and I asked my skipper for an hour off, so I went home at 1pm. Later, on the news, I saw a report about a police officer being shot. I am not going to give you the details, but if I had not asked for the time off then I would have been the first officer on the scene. It was on my area and I would have been the first car deployed to what was reported as a domestic. The officer that did get there first was shot in the leg and his police dog was killed trying to protect him. The officer did survive, although it could have been another Hungerford massacre, some of you will recall this tragic event from 1987.

Enough said I think.

Michael Wood

Protective equipment

One thing that did help with the reports of violence and the fights we attended on a Friday or Saturday was the PR24, an American side handled baton. With the correct training, we could take control of a fight and protect ourselves. That thought made me feel a lot better and I was beginning to get my confidence back, beginning to like the job again. Just a little though. I still ran every day's events through my mind, painfully, when I got back home after work

I went to a lot of fights during my service, some minor, some major, too many to mention them all, but I am going to mention some that scared me, some that I still think about even though I have long left the job. You also get some idiots that want to fight for no reason. They will try and wind you up, make you lose your temper and snap, so they can then make a complaint against you if you hit them.

I saw a couple of incidents where this had happened, and papers were served on the officers involved. I had papers served on me after a major fight in the town one night. In fact, I think possibly every officer there had a complaint made against him or her from this particular person.

It was a Saturday night and the town was full. There were about five of us in a van, driving around in case of trouble. There was a call for assistance over the radio and we made our way to the local taxi office. When we got there, it was mayhem. There were about twenty people in the doorway of the office shouting and screaming at something inside.

That something was the officer who had asked for assistance. He was trying to arrest someone. We all managed to get into the office and start ejecting people. Some were arrested, others were told to go home. I stood in the doorway of the office with my PR24 out, holding it across my chest with both hands, keeping people out.

Michael Wood

All of a sudden I saw this huge man pushing his way through the crowd in front of me. He got up to me and tried to push past. I managed to hold him back a bit, but he was too strong. He told me to let him past or he would knock me out. He threw a punch. I ducked and he was past. I managed to get in front of him again and put my baton against his chest and started pushing him back. He said that he was doorman and started pushing me backwards. All hell broke loose then. There was a massive punch up outside, involving all twenty or so of the original crowd, us half-a-dozen police officers, plus reinforcements summoned from all over the county. This resulted in me and several others being served papers of a complaint a few days later. More stress for me and other officers to deal with.

You always had stress, some could manage it, and some couldn't. I was one of them that couldn't

Things went downhill from there. I was working long hours and seeing less of my wife and family. A couple of incidents had me working 23hrs one Friday, 16hrs on the Saturday and 12hrs the Sunday. Back for a quick change over to the Monday early shift.

As a result my wife left me. She had no contact with me for three weeks. I was devastated. I had the kids to look after and my work. About three weeks later I received divorce papers through the post. The reason given in the divorce papers was unreasonable behaviour. Now that covers a multitude of things, but the one sole thing that wrecked my first marriage was the drink. Why did I drink? I drank to forget, not an excuse I know but at the time it helped me sleep without the dreams, not all the time though.

I was single again and settled into a routine of going to work, coming home cooking the kids dinner and myself, watching TV and going to bed. The kids, having grown up, then started to move out and I was eventually on my own in this big house. Because of the divorce, I had to take out an IVA (Individual Voluntary Arrangement) to clear the £35,000 of debts that we had.

Michael Wood

I had to take out an IVA because police officers cannot legally be declared bankrupt but debts still have to be cleared. Under an IVA, you cannot borrow money, use a credit card, chequebook or even open standard current bank account.

I had to sell my car because I couldn't afford to run it. I had to account for every penny for five years! Before I took out the IVA, my mum had cleared one of the credit cards for me. I didn't tell the people who did my IVA that I had a clear credit card. I needed that for emergencies.

I had a small motorbike for getting to and from work, and used it in all weathers. On reflection, I think I must have been going through a mid life crisis. The small bike wasn't fast enough, so I took my test and got a big, old, Kawasaki GPZ 1100. Now that was a fast bike, but as I said it was old. When I used to go out on bike rides with my mates I had a job keeping up with them on the winding roads, mainly due to the fact that they had new modern bikes with better tyres that enabled them to go round corners quicker. Then one day on the way to work I blew the engine up. Back to the little 125 again. I tried on loads of occasions to get a new bike on credit, but because of the IVA my credit rating was rock bottom.

So I asked my eldest son Anthony if he would take a loan out for me and I would pay him back. He agreed and I went looking for a new bike. When I found the bike I was looking for, everything went up a notch. I brought a Honda Fireblade. Because I had the 'Blade' I had to get leathers to match the colours of the machine. When I wasn't working, I was always out on the bike.

But my mind still wasn't right. I could remember coming back from some bike rides, sitting down and going through the whole ride in my head.
Once again thinking what would have happened if I had overtaken the car sooner or gone round that bend faster or slower.

Writing that last sentence has brought another incident to mind.

Michael Wood

Pythonesque

Remember I mentioned the problems of people having a go at you, even though you are trying to help them. This incident has just come to mind. It was about 10.30 in the evening and I was sent to the report of an accident, motorbike verses car. Now all the time you're en route to an accident involving a cyclist or motorcyclist, you fear the worse case scenario, cars normally win.

I got to the scene and saw a person in the middle of the road trying to get up. He had no crash helmet on and just normal clothing. There was blood everywhere, at first I thought he might have been a pedestrian that had been hit by the bike or car. But it turned out to be the rider of the bike. The reason he couldn't stand was due to the fact he only had one and a half legs.

One of his legs had been snapped off just below the knee on impact with the parked car he had hit. He thought he still had a leg as he could see it, but it was only still there because it was inside the leg of his jeans and they were only hanging on by a thread at the back of the leg.

The ambulance hadn't arrived yet, so I got out to try and give him first aid. He then started fighting me, trying to kick me. The only problem was, he was trying to kick me with the leg that had been snapped off and he was just throwing blood everywhere. The ambulance arrived and the paramedics took over. I started then to investigate the scene. It turned out the youth had just stolen the bike and come down the road too fast, lost control and hit the parked car, no crash helmet on, no leathers, no protection at all.

He was lucky to be alive and as far as I know he still steals bikes and cars even with a false leg. On the way home that night, on my bike I rode slower than I used to, not because I had seen the result of a bike accident, it was because I was thinking, great that's another one to dream about and I did.

Michael Wood

Second Wife and back to Northampton

It was during this time that I met Ruth, my second wife. She was and still is a diamond, during the period of five years of the IVA Ruth used, to help me out with money if I got short one month. I used to ask her to borrow money some months and others she would just give me some, or she would pay for some food if we went to the shops. Ruth used to stop some nights and others I would walk her home as she lived in the same village.

I can remember the first time I met Ruth. It was in the village pub. As I have said, I got myself into a routine after the divorce. I used to go down the pub some nights, most nights, and I was always there on Sunday lunchtime. I used to go in and sit at the bar on a stool facing the door so I could see everybody that came into the pub. I can remember sitting there one night and Ruth was sat at a table with her mates. I didn't know it then, but I do now, that some of them fancied me.

But as Ruth would tell you now, I wouldn't know if a female were coming onto me, I wouldn't have a clue. As I have said, because of the IVA, I used to watch all the pennies and if I went to the pub I would only spend my allowance and leave. Ruth came up to the bar to get another drink and asked me if I wanted one. I declined and said, "No thanks, I can't return the favour." She insisted and things progressed from there.

When I first met Ruth I was working back at Northampton. I had to leave the Wellingborough area because I had a fling with my best mates wife. It was a lot more than that but I won't go into details and if my old best mate is reading this, sorry is all I can say.

Working back at Northampton started off well I was able to meet up again with all the people I had started with. I was doing the same job, IRV work, going to domestics, accidents, fights, and all the everyday stuff. Now working back at Northampton was an eye opener once again. B and because it was the county town and the largest town, most of the trouble you went to was on a larger

82

Scale. You were always busy and there was always plenty of paperwork. I was beginning to get stressed again

Ruth moved in with me into the police house. I then changed role and became a community beat officer. I had got fed up with attending accidents and domestics all the time. My hands were also giving me problems and I was diagnosed with Tenosynivitus (inflammation of the tendons in the hands) that made it difficult to grab hold of a prisoner and keep hold.

Although at the time I didn't mention it to my bosses too much. When Ruth moved in, she also had with her a shy little girl called Kayleigh, her daughter, who I now see as my own daughter. Kay, as we call her now, wouldn't talk to me and spent most of her time in her bedroom. Ruth also had two other children, Stacey and Scott. I will speak more about them later.

So there I was, I had ditched the police car and I was walking the beat again. I had my own little area that I walked every day. I visited the two lower (primary) schools in the area and gave talks to the kids, went to council meetings and tried to implement changes so that the area was a safer place. I was enjoying myself and the job was more relaxed, at first.

It was whilst doing this job that I saw an advert in the paper. All it said was 'ride a bike in Brazil' and a phone number. I phoned the number and it was the charity Lepra. Basically, I had to organise some sponsorship for the flights and accommodation and then get sponsor money to give to the charity for the treatment of the disease Leprosy. And, of course, ride a bicycle (not a motorbike!) 340 miles around Brazil.

Before I approached some companies for sponsorship, I did some research into the disease, as I wanted to be armed with enough information to get the message across.

I didn't realise that no one knows how people catch Leprosy but it can be cured at a cost of £21.00. That's how much a course of drugs costs for each person. So off I went, found a local company to sponsor me and spent two weeks of my leave cycling around the mountain region of Natal in northern Brazil. I had a great time and lost a lot of weight.

When I returned from Brazil, there were some changes made to the way we worked the area. Three of us were given an off road motorbike. We did all the correct training with man who used to be a champion of the sport and also a police motorbike course so we could ride the bikes on the road. We also of course could chase stolen motorbikes across sports fields and other rough ground.

The three of us used to go out and try and catch the stolen bikes that were ridden around the estates of Northampton, not just in my own area. The success rate was good and we were getting a name for ourselves, so much so that we were called upon to do a lot of work with other departments. Sometimes we would be on standby for special operations, if there were the possibility that some criminals would drive or ride off road. It became more demanding and over time I realised that I didn't want to do it any more.

Depression

All of a sudden it hit me, and I cannot remember why, or how. But on the 8th September 1996 I was sitting at home and I thought I was having a heart attack, although I wasn't sure. I jumped in the car and drove myself to casualty. Once I was there, they put me on a cardiograph machine and did a load more tests. It turned out to be an anxiety and panic attack. There had been a couple of incidents that made me very depressed and anxious but I can't remember them now. As a result I had about 10 months off sick. During the time I was off I saw a shrink, who managed to reduce me to tears by the end of each session. He was very good and said it could be post-traumatic stress that I was suffering. I didn't care what he thought; all I wanted to do was leave the police.

Michael Wood

If I saw a police car I used to panic and go all sweaty, so I asked for a medical pension and early retirement.

I just couldn't leave. I only had about 6 years of service left and if I left now I would lose about £40,000 of my pension. As I have said, I was in the job for the pension.

So it was a case of 'string it along' for as long as possible. After the 10 months off sick, I was told to come back to work or resign. Now I wasn't about to resign, so I went back to work.

When it was time to go back to work I was on restricted duties, which meant I could go back to work and if I felt that I couldn't cope after an hour I was allowed to go home. I gradually increased my hours to the maximum of eight per day. I had 5 years of service left and I didn't want to work on the streets again. I was conscious of the growing pressure on the police to be politically correct and that anything you did as a police officer could land you in deep crap if the person making the complaint knew how to work the system.

I just didn't want to be police officer any more and definitely didn't want to go on the street again, so I brought my hands into play and said that I was finding it difficult to hold a police baton. I thought even then, that I was going to milk this and in the next 5 years of service have as much time off sick has possible due the problems with my hands.

The first part of the plan worked. The police doctor, who was very good, then put me on restricted duties for the rest of my service due to my hands. He said to the bosses that I was unable to hold a baton for self-defence work or grip a person hard and long enough to affect an arrest.

Michael Wood

Back to work after ten months off

So I was shown into a room by the station Sergeant, who told me
set up a help desk where members of the public could phone up
for advice on law, criminal, civil, or even matrimonial. Actually,
any type of law you could think of. So a mate of mine who was
also on restricted duties joined me in setting up the help desk.
We took a lot of work from the control room and allowed them to
get on with the real job of policing. Before we set up the help
desk, the control room staff had to sit there for twenty or thirty
minutes talking to people giving them advice while still
controlling incidents on the street. In a way we were doing a good
job.

But, what I found amazing was the fact that as we got more and
more phone calls about advice I started to remember a lot that I
had learnt over the years and it was a very rewarding job. Then it
became boring and stressful, as the people phoning wouldn't
listen to what I was saying to them and they started making
complaints. Of course, if a complaint is made about an officer
then the discipline department got involved and you could be
suspended. Once again, I was becoming depressed and took
some time off work. It got to the point where I wasn't sleeping
and drinking more and more. I still drink too much now, but not
as much as I used to.

The one person who gave me lots of support and understanding
was Ruth. At the time she was excellent, and still is. She used to
wake up some mornings and ask whom I had been chasing in my
dreams, as my arms and legs had been moving about so much in
my sleep. Most of the times I couldn't, or perhaps wouldn't,
remember my dreams.

But one thing I did know was that I was becoming ill again and I
went to see my doctor. He asked me if I was as bad as the last
time when I had taken ten months off. I said no. He still gave me
some anti-depressants, which I didn't take. In fact, all the time I
had off sick with stress or depression over the years, I never took
a single tablet. You hear so many stories about people becoming

addicted to the drugs their own doctor prescribes them. I thought I didn't want to become one of them.

Scott, my stepson, Ruth's son was a bit of a rebel when he was sixteen or seventeen. He was one of the youths of today who think they know the law and he was always getting into trouble, not just for his driving offences on motorbikes, but with the other local youths. Scott slowly moved into the house with Ruth, Kay and myself. Ruth knew that we didn't get on, and I think that was due to the fact that I was a copper.

So we let him stay the odd night on the settee. After a little time had passed, he had nowhere else to stay, so we agreed that he would sleep in a caravan on the drive. So we bought a second hand caravan and he stayed in there. Then the stress really started building up for all of us, not because he was there or because of his attitude towards life in general, it was because of the trouble he used to bring home. I don't blame him though, it was only because he was still a kid and hadn't grown up yet.

At the time I couldn't care less what he did as long as it didn't affect my job and most of all, my entire pension.

He used to have a falling out with most people as he used to borrow money that he knew he couldn't pay back. Sometimes we used to get youths turning up on the doorstep causing problems.

It got so bad at one point that we were given a police radio to call for help if we needed it at night.

Now don't get me wrong, I didn't dislike Scott as a person, because sometimes he would be very helpful and do anything you asked of him. It was just the fact that he was still a kid and immature and wouldn't listen most of the time. He thought he was right and the rest of the world was wrong.

He would do anything for anybody, except his mum that is. At the time that was his major failing. Now, years on, he is a father and a good father, to our grandson Oliver. He still has a few problems but I think, all in all, he is slowly getting his act together. Now I promised Ruth that I wouldn't slag Scott off in this book, mainly because I believe it would detrimental to Scott as a man that he now is.

I began dreaming again, only this time the dreams were a lot worse. I would go to sleep and it was the same dream every night. I would dream that I was in the station yard, sitting in the police car. I would then drive out and go a certain route. Each night each route out would be different. But whichever route I took, the journey was halted when I got to the scene of a bad accident. I then relived the whole accident, the condition of the vehicles, the people involved and the injuries sustained. I didn't like it.

It got so bad that sometimes during the day when I was out driving, even off-duty and passed a location of a bad accident, I was doing the same. I was also silently crying to myself. I knew I was getting bad, but I didn't want to admit it to myself or anyone else. Even sitting here now typing, when I am retired, I can still see the bad ones.

One thing I can remember doing will always stay with me. It was the night before the funeral of Princess Diana, in October 1995. I actually sat at the place she was going to be buried, on the Island at the Althrop Estate. My job was to guard the Island from any press that were trying to get to the place for photographs. It was quite eerie, knowing that Princess Diana was to be laid to rest there. But I had a job to do. We did catch one member of the press who had got into the grounds, but he hadn't got any where near to the Island.

There were a couple of incidents in the village that put me off sick also. Scott, my stepson, used to have some mates in the caravan with him. Sometimes, Ruth and I didn't mind this, as we knew where they all were. One day however, I was looking out of the window and I saw one of the youths leave the caravan with a quilt under his arm. Now I hated the youth in question and had banned him from the house loads of times, but he just ignored me. I didn't want to press the matter at the time because I was close to retirement, only about 2 years left and I wanted my pension.

But, on this occasion I couldn't look the other way. He had stolen something of mine and was walking down the street with it. I caught up with him and told him he was under arrest for theft, marched him back to the house, locked him the office and called the police. Now the police house years ago used to be a village Police Station. There was a main door from the path that leads into an office, where the village bobby could take details of crimes etc. There was then another front door that leads into the house itself; effectively there were two front doors.

So, I locked this youth in the office and waited for the police to arrive. But he had a mobile phone on him and he phoned his father at the other end of the village. Before the local police arrived, the father turned up, attacked me and took his son aside and waited for the police to get there.

When the local officers arrived, all I could hear were the words 'assault and false imprisonment', committed of course by me!

Well that put me right over the edge. I could see myself being suspended, taken to court, losing my job and also my pension.

Ruth was fantastic; she got me through it all and out of the other side. But at the time I was in a bad way, I was due to appear in Crown Court a few days after the incident but I was sick.

The judge in the case insisted that I attend the court hearing. After a few phone calls, a senior officer was sent to my house to see me. Once he saw the state of me, he contacted the court and said there was no way I could attend and that there was no way I could take any questions from any barrister there. The case went on without me. I was a mental wreck. I couldn't stop crying and if I saw a police uniform I started shaking. I saw the doctor and he said if I didn't see a shrink there and then, I would have a total breakdown.

Michael Wood

I was booked off as long term sick again. Now, I cannot
remember if the other incident took place whilst I was off sick or
when I got back to work, but the caravan blew up one afternoon
with a load of kids inside. Ruth and I were in the house. We heard
a loud bang and saw flames coming out of the caravan. We also
saw the kids diving out of it, some from the windows and some
from the door. It was Ruth that called the Fire Brigade and
Ambulance.

That wasn't too stressful until all the agencies started arriving.
Some of the kids were badly burnt, including Scott. The skin had
peeled off his hands. The fire brigade arrived and put the fire out.
I stopped in the house, I couldn't go out, and I was too scared.
Yet, years ago, I would have been the first one out there giving
first aid. I just kept thinking what's going to happen now?

The welfare department of the force was very good. They
organised for me to see a shrink. I saw her once a week for five
weeks, after which see said I needed more and she was going to
ask the force to pay for another five sessions, which they did. The
very first session was quite mild; she didn't press my mind too
much and asked just a few basic questions about my life in
general.

I can remember I was sitting in a small office in her house. It was
small back bedroom and all it contained were two armchairs, a
desk and a small table next to my chair. On the table next to me
was a box of tissues. I got through a lot of tissues during our
sessions. One of the walls was lined with a bookshelf and I can
remember seeing that it contained book after book about
psychology, the mind and all things like that.

When I told her about my recurring dream, she asked me to write
a letter when I got home. She wanted me to write to three dead
people. I chose three but wrote just one letter to all of them.

Now, I cannot remember what I wrote but what I can remember is
at the time of writing it I couldn't stop crying, crying is not a
strong enough word: I actually sobbed my heart out. As I did

when I read the letter back to her on the next session. But it actually helped.

During the sessions we talked about my dreams, about what I felt after each incident that seemed to affect me more than others. The talking helped and the bad dreams started to fade away. She diagnosed me as suffering with post-traumatic stress disorder. She said that it might never go away, but that it should ease when I retired from the police.

I returned to work about three months later, in November 2005, with about eighteen months left to serve. Once again, I was not on a full shift straight away. I was eased back into the help desk and back to the phone calls and other stuff.

Family

Ruth and I were married on 18th October 2003. It was a wonderful day, all the family were there and it was a GOOD day. Let me just tell you about my family: my wife is a few years younger than me. She is good looking (although she would say she isn't and that I am biased) hard working, and would do anything for anybody. I just wish she was here with me now, but circumstances prevent that at the moment.

Now let's mention the kids, as they say on TV and in no particular order.

Stacey is second oldest of my three daughters. I don't know how she copes. She has just completed her degree. She got married this year on the 18th October 2008 to Nathan. They gave Ruth and I our first grandchild, Niamh. Now Stacey's wedding, in a way, was a sad day for me. I look on Stacey as my own daughter and I wanted to stand in the front of the church and be with her when she signed the marriage certificate. I know I couldn't, as she had to have her natural father up there, but it didn't stop me wanting to be there. I did shed a small tear in the church.

Michael Wood

I thought no one had seen me but I was wrong. Kay, the youngest, had seen the tear and said she so to me afterwards. While Stacey was doing her degree, she was holding down three jobs, going to college, looking after her daughter and keeping house as well. She now has a full time job within her chosen subject from college. This was Criminology and Sociology, would you believe it! She is going to go a long way, as she is a hard worker. She is also an excellent mother, just like her own.

Kayleigh (Kay) lives with her partner Robert and they have just had our third grandchild, Ryan. Kay never used to speak to me much, when we lived in the police house, but over the years we have got close and now she speaks all the time and calls me dad. I would be honoured to walk Kay down the aisle when she gets married, as I would have Stacey, but I know that will never happen. I would feel uncomfortable about doing it, only because the natural father would have to be there to sign the certificate. So, I will leave the honour to my wife again, but once more I shall probably shed a silent tear and hope no one sees it. Kay is going to be a strict mother like Stacey and another excellent one.

Melanie, my third daughter, is living with her partner. She phoned me one day to tell she was pregnant. By the time you read this, I will be a grandfather for fourth time! Now I have the same problem with Mel as I had with Stacey and will have with Kay. I won't be able to sign the certificate as her natural father will have to do it, although I brought Mel up as my own from the age of two. I won't even get the chance to walk her down the aisle, so I have three daughters who I am proud of and love. At least it lets me off the hook when it comes to the speeches at the weddings, because I know it would be hard for me not to shed a tear or two.

Now for the boys. Scott, as I have said already, is my stepson. I am not going to call him my son, because he wouldn't want me to. When he talks about me to people he always calls me his step-dad. Scott lives with his partner and they produced our second grandchild Oliver. Now, Oliver is an excellent baby, the same as Scott is an excellent father. Scott is also a hard worker, when he goes to work. I am sure in years to come Scott will prove us all wrong, and if you are reading this Scott, please do it.

Anthony, my eldest son from my first marriage, rents his mothers house and is training to be a teacher. Who in their right mind would want to be a teacher these days? They have more constraints than the police, but that's the path he has chosen and good luck to him. He is going to find it hard dealing with the youth of today.

Ryan, my youngest son, is a hairdresser. I should really use the word stylist, not hairdresser. He is good at his job and I would say one of the best at the salon where he works. Everybody likes Ryan; all the women that see him have the hots for him. Sometimes he gets embarrassed about this, because the females actually tell him to his face.

Michael Wood

Back to the help desk and towards the end

Now where was I, back to work in the help desk in November 2005 as I said? You might think that the job of answering the phone all day is not stressful, well it is. You get annoyed and frustrated at some of the callers because they won't listen if they don't like the advice you give them. They are on the phone straight away to the boss and the first you know of it is when the boss walks into the office and says, "I have just had Mr or Mrs so and so on the phone. Tell me about it." You tell him and at the end he says, "Do me a favour, phone them back and apologise." Apologise, I would say, what for, I haven't done anything wrong. That's when the anger and frustration starts turning into stress.

There was a lighter side of this particular job. You always knew if there had been a fictional programme on the TV the night before, one that involved spies and gadgets.

You get phone calls from people asking you to bug someone's car or house, or locate where they are going by following the signal from their mobile phone. Some of the things you see on TV can be done, but I am not going to say what, as I signed the Official Secrets Act when I joined the army and the police.

Another day, another suicide

I dreamt last night and it wasn't a good one. It was about another incident I went to, but the dream had a different outcome to the real thing.

I had to complete your pocket notebook as soon as possible after an incident. But, if nothing much happened, I would wait a couple hours and write up the events in one go. I can remember a particular time when I was writing up my book. It was about four in the morning one summer and it was just beginning to get light. I had decided to drive out of town and park up in a gateway to a field, to get some peace and quiet.

Michael Wood

As I was doing this, a couple of cars went by but I paid them no attention, my head was down writing in my book. I then received a message over the radio. Could I please get to a phone as soon as possible and phone in. Now if you get a message like that you know that something serious could have happened, the details of which that could not be broadcast over the radio.

I drove to a small hamlet where I knew there was a phone box. I called the control room and the job that I was given filled me with horror. A woman said she was driving home and she had found a policeman dead in a police car. The location given was about half a mile from where I was making the phone call.

All the thoughts of me driving away to Norfolk that day came back to me, when I was looking for a place to contemplate suicide and I thought this man has done it in a police car. I didn't want to go to the job, but I knew I had to. As I was on the way, I started to get angry rather than scared. Shit, I thought, does this man realise how much paperwork is involved in a suicide? I answered that question myself. Of course he did, he was a policeman. So there I was, driving slowly down the road, looking for two cars, one with a distraught woman in and a police car with a body in.

Something happened then that eased my worries a bit, but not a lot though. I crossed the county boundary into Bedfordshire. I informed control of this and a few minutes later found the distraught woman in her car but no police car. There was another car there and it did contain a man that had gassed himself, as I could see the hose from the exhaust into the window. He was not a policeman.

I asked for Bedfordshire police to attend, then talked to the woman.
My first question to her was, "Why did you say it was policeman dead in a car when you first phoned"?

She replied " I don't know, that's the last thing I remember seeing, a policeman in a car with his head down."

Michael Wood

We then came to the same conclusion. She had driven past me as I was writing up my book and then came across the dead man in the car. The shock of finding the man had pushed the last thing she saw to the front of her mind and that had been me sitting in my car.

The mind, it's amazing what the mind does to you. I dreamt of that incident one night, three months after I started writing this book. But in my dream I was in the car and the woman had found me.

I can remember now going back home that morning and not being able to sleep, just sitting down in the chair watching TV and having a drink.

Where was I?

One of the jobs that we decided to take on in the help desk was nuisance phone calls. At first it was just give advice about contacting the phone company concerned and giving the caller a reference number.

We then started to really get involved with the jobs of nuisance phone calls and we became curious as to what could be done. You will be amazed what can be done and what we, the Police, can find out about a mobile phone from the moment it's turned on from new. For example, even when delete your text messages, they will almost certainly stay on your SIM card for a very, very, long time. Devices exist which can bring these back!

The last word?

This story I hope to continue but also include other events of the first 17 years of my service, rather than the last five, which were so much of a problem.

Now I am not an expert in book writing. I have just tried to put down in words how I have felt over the years. It's about how I got to where I am now, on a balcony in Portugal on my own.

96

Michael Wood

Drink wrecked my first marriage and it's not having a good effect on my second marriage at the moment. Now, I don't get drunk every night, but the amount of drink I do have is having an effect on my relationship with Ruth. That's why I am here and she is back in England. Now I can hear you saying, well get back home and sort it out.

It's not that easy. Since I have retired from the police, the only work I have been able to find is part time work. I can only earn just enough money to pay the bills.

To be perfectly honest I do not know what the future holds for me.

Apart from work, sleep and work again and probably dying a lonely old man.

Now the tears have started, perhaps the doctors and shrinks were wrong.

Perhaps I will never get better.

That's what being a police officer has done for me.

Michael Wood

That's me on the front cover, this is a short story about me, its about the highs and lows of being a modern police officer. About what I saw during 22 years of service.
"Not a mark on her, not a sign of any blood, nothing, she was DEAD"
" I fell over the second body flat on my face, at this stage I started to panic."
I hope it will give you the reader a little insight about the role of a police officer. Perhaps then you will also realise that not all police officers are the tough macho men or women you think we are.

We just have to give you. THE PUBLIC.
The impression that we are.